Grammar Springboards

The fun teaching resource that enables children
to jump ahead in grammar

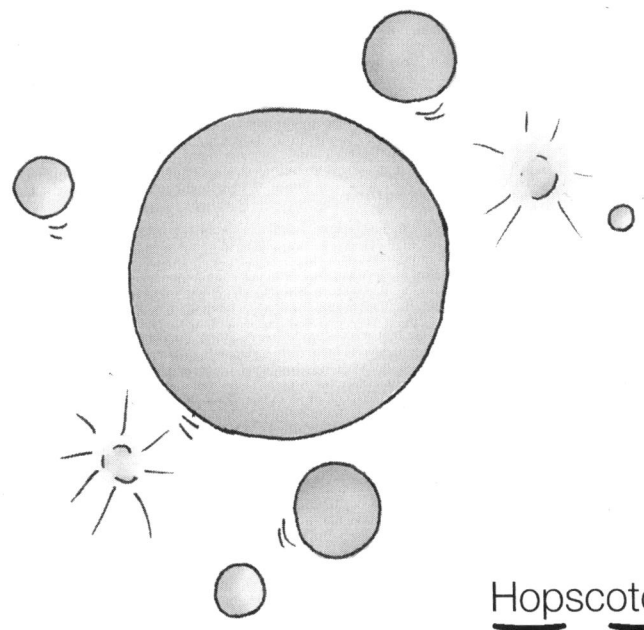

Alison Milford

Hopscotch

A division of MA Education Ltd

Hopscotch

A division of MA Education Ltd

Published by Hopscotch, a division of
MA Education, St Jude's Church,
Dulwich Road, London, SE24 0PB
www.hopscotchbooks.com
020 7738 5454

First edition © MA Education 2010.
Second edition © MA Education 2014.

Written by Alison Milford

Designed by Fonthill Creative, 01722 717057

Illustrated by Emma Turner

ISBN 978 1 909860 21 6

Contents

Introduction 6

Chapter 1 – Nouns
Noun information 8
Objective chart 9
Noun springboards 10
Lesson plans and activities:
• Common nouns 11
• Proper nouns 16
• Plural noun suffixes '-s' and '-es' 21
• Compound nouns 26
• Making nouns with suffixes 30
• Expanded noun phrases 35

Chapter 2 – Pronouns
Pronoun information 40
Objective chart 41
Pronoun springboards 42
Lesson plans and activities:
• Singular pronouns 43
• Plural pronouns 48

Chapter 3 – Verbs
Verb information 54
Objective chart 56
Verb springboards 57
Lesson plans and activities:
• Action verbs 58
• Past tense verbs ending in '-ed' or '-d' 63
• Present tense verbs ending in '-ing' 68
• Verbs starting with 'un-' prefix 72
• Irregular verbs 77

Chapter 4 – Adjectives
Adjective information 84
Objective chart 86
Adjective springboards 87
Lesson plans and activities:
• Descriptive adjectives 1 – settings 88
• Descriptive adjectives 2 – people 92
• Changing adjectives with prefix 'un-' 98
• Making adjectives using suffixes '-ful', '-less' 102
• Making adverbs from adjectives using '-ly' 107
• Use of suffixes '-er' and '-est' 112

Chapter 5 – Sentences
Sentence information 117
Objective chart 118
Sentence springboards 119
Lesson plans and activities:
• Simple sentences 120
• Co-ordination in sentences 125
• Subordination in sentences 130
• Simple time connectives 135

Chapter 6 – Punctuation
Punctuation information 141
Objective chart 143
Punctuation springboards 144
Lesson plans and activities:
• Sentence punctuation – capitals, full stops, exclamation marks 145
• Questions 150
• Commas in lists 156
• Apostrophes 163

Assessment
Periodic Assessment tests
(two levelled tests for each subject) 168
Transitional Assessment tests (two levelled tests) 193

CD-ROM

Lesson resources

Worksheets
(Two levelled worksheets per grammar subject)
Nouns
Pronouns
Verbs
Adjectives
Sentences
Punctuation

Records for assessment
Individual grammar record sheet
Group activity record
Group record sheets (one per grammar subject)
My grammar target record sheets (two levelled tests)

Teacher resources
Word bank
Speech bubble template
Word web
Word search grids 1 and 2
Mini book and Zig-Zag book templates
Star puzzle template
The word ladder
Word wall blank flash cards
Grammar badges
Book marks
Story 'Nothing much'
Word wheel – blank
Word wheel cover – one blank/one decorated
Word slides – template
Word slide book
Word searches

Introduction

About the series

Grammar Springboards is a series of three attractive resource books and CD-ROMs designed to make grammar a stimulating and fun learning experience for children of all abilities within KS1 and KS2. Each book is closely linked to the New National Curriculum of 2014's Programmes of Study and the statutory English Appendix 2: Vocabulary, grammar and punctuation.

Together, the books and the CD-ROMs make an excellent tool for:

- Teaching grammar in a range of class settings, as lessons, within groups, individually or as homework.

- Teachers and teaching assistants to access easy to use resources and activities for different class situations.

- Using elements from the New National Curriculum of 2014's Programmes of Study and the statutory 'English Appendix 2: Vocabulary, grammar and punctuation'.

- Pupil assessment with opportunities for day to day assessment, periodic assessment and transitional assessment.

About the book

Each book focuses on the main areas of grammar taught within KS1 and KS2.

These are:

- Nouns

- Pronouns

- Verbs

- Adjectives

- Sentences

- Punctuation.

There are three main sections to the book:

Section 1

Section 1 is set out in chapters covering each of the main grammar areas – nouns, pronouns, verbs, adjectives, sentences, punctuation.

Each chapter contains:

Grammar information: Teacher information about the uses and different aspects of the grammar subject, including a glossary of terms, examples and word tables.

Grammar and punctuation objective chart: A simple to read chart to show what grammar and punctuation objectives are covered in the grammar lessons and activities.

Ideas springboard: Fun ideas for wall displays, games and activities for the class, groups or individuals. Some resources for games and activities can be found in 'Teacher resources' – on the CD-ROM.

Lesson plans: Suggested lesson plans for the different grammar subjects and objectives, e.g. 'Chapter 1 – Nouns' includes the subjects Common nouns, Proper nouns and Compound nouns.

Each lesson has a main teacher led lesson followed by differentiated activities for three ability groups.

Each lesson plan has:

* **Lesson objectives**

* **Resources:** list of suggested resources for the lesson and activities. Resources can be found in 'Lesson resources' on the CD-ROM.

* **Lesson/activity notes:** Suggestions on setting up resources and suggested grouping and support for the activity groups.

* **Introduction:** Ideas for introducing a grammar subject.

* **Main lesson:** Teacher or adult led lesson with class participation.

* **Differentiated group activities:** Three bullet point activities.

* **Plenary:** Suggestions on ways to reinforce the lessons objectives.

* **Support:** Ideas for supporting children who may need more reinforcement or consolidation in their learning.

* **Extension:** Ideas and challenges for children who have grasped the main objectives and need to extend their knowledge.

* **Activity worksheets or resources:** The activity worksheets are set out in age related abilities from Year 1 to end of Year 2.

Section 2: Assessment

Periodic Assessment tests: Two levelled short tests to accompany each grammar chapter. The questions cover all the grammar areas taught in each chapter.

Transitional Assessment tests: Two levelled transitional tests that can be used at the end of a school year to judge the progress and understanding of grammar subjects.

Section 3: CD-ROM

The accompanying CD-ROM contains resources which can be used on whiteboards, printed or photocopied.

Lesson resources: Include resources to accompany each of the lesson plans, including texts to highlight or re-model word and sentence examples, flashcards, information posters, games, templates for word sliders and pictures.

Worksheets: Stand alone worksheets for reinforcement, extension, homework and individual assessment. There are two levelled worksheets linked to each grammar subject covered within each chapter.

Records for assessment:

* **Individual Grammar Record Sheet:** To be used during an activity for observing or assessing a child's responses and understanding of the objective.

* **Group Activity Record:** To be used for writing observational notes and the children's comments during a group activity.

* **Group Record Charts:** To be used to record when certain children in a specific group have understood different learning objectives.

* **My grammar target record sheet:** A child's own record sheet of achieving the learning objectives of the different grammar subjects. There is one sheet per grammar subject with a tick chart and a design to colour in as children achieve each objective.

Teacher resources:

* Word bank

* Word searches and word search grid templates

* Templates for models and games

* Definitions posters

* Flash cards

* Fun grammar book marks and badges.

Word Bank: This useful resource can be used by teachers as a quick and easy reference or by children exploring different words and creating their own word banks.

Chapter 1 – Nouns
Noun information

Common noun	A word that is used to name people, places, objects or creatures.	*clown, fire–fighter, forest, airport, pen, strawberry, tiger, grasshopper*
Proper noun	A word that gives people, places, objects and events their specific or special names. Proper nouns always begin with a capital letter.	*Mr Benson, Mrs Khan, Doctor Lee, Queen's Avenue, Tesco, Arsenal Football Club, River Thames, Cardiff, Fife, Saturn, Snickers, Monday, April, France*
Compound noun	A word made up of two nouns.	*snowman, teabag, peanut, sunflower, rainbow, toothbrush, suitcase, footpath*
Singular noun	A noun that names one person, place, object or creature.	*castle, shell, flag, bucket, bird, spade, crab, towel*
Plural noun	A noun that names more than one person, place, object or creature. Most plural nouns are created by adding '-s' on the end.	*castles, shells, flags, buckets, birds, spades, crabs, towels*
	To make singular nouns that end with the letters x, ch, sh, ss into plural nouns, add '-es' on the end.	*dresses, foxes, beaches, brushes*
	Some nouns are both singular and plural.	*sand, sheep, seaweed, deer, trousers, scissors*
	For singular nouns that end in '-y', change the '-y' to '-i' before '-es' is added.	*fly – flies, baby – babies*
Making nouns with suffixes '-ment', '-ness'	Nouns can sometimes be made by attaching suffixes to verbs and adjectives. Add the suffix onto the end of the root word, for example: *pavement, sadness*. If the root word has more than one syllable and ends in '-y' with a consonant before it, then change the '-y' to '-i' and then add the suffixes.	*happy – happiness, merry – merriment*
Making nouns with the suffix '-er'	Nouns can sometimes be made when adding '-er' to verbs. If the verb ends with an '-e', drop the '-e' before adding '-er'.	*build – builder, write – writer*
Expanded noun phrases	A noun phrase is a phrase that gives information about a main noun by using words such as verbs, adjectives, adverbs, prepositions and other nouns to describe it and specify where it is. They can be as short as one-word phrases or longer. Information can be added in front of the main noun and after the main noun.	*The crazy cat jumped into the deep well*.

Noun objective chart

Objectives	Common nouns	Proper nouns	Plural noun suffixes '-s' and '-es'	Compound nouns	Making nouns with suffixes	Expanded noun phrases
Word – Year 1						
Recognise nouns.	★	★	★	★	★	★
Regular plural noun suffixes '-s' or '-es'.			★			
Suffixes that can be added to verbs '-er'.					★	
Recognise singular and plural nouns.			★			
Word – Year 2						
Use nouns.	★	★	★	★	★	★
Use adjectives.						★
Use singular and plural nouns.			★		★	★
Formation of nouns using suffixes such as '-ness', '-ment', '-er'.					★	
Formation of nouns by compounding.				★		
Sentence – Year 1						
How words can combine to make sentences.	★					
Joining words and joining clauses using 'and'.	★					
Sentence – Year 2						
Expanded noun phrases.						★
Different sentences: Statement, question, exclamation, command.	★	★	★	★	★	★
Text – Year 1						
Sequencing sentences to form short narrative.			★			
Text – Year 2						
Use of present and past tense in writing.			★			★
Punctuation – Year 1						
Capital letters, full stops, question marks, exclamation marks to demarcate sentences.		★				
Capital letters for names and for the personal pronoun 'I'.		★				
Punctuation – Year 2						
Capital letters, full stops, question marks, exclamation marks to demarcate sentences.		★			★	

Noun springboards

Noun ideas

Collect catalogues, brochures and magazines that include examples of the four types of common nouns. Give a group of children one noun category such as 'people' and ask them to cut them out. Let them create labels and display their nouns with the labels as a display.

Let the children research a noun category. For example they can discuss and find out more about people's jobs and their titles, *firefighter*, *doctor*, *teacher*. A class noun list of the workers' names can be added onto the board with labels and information about the jobs.

Create graphs from a survey and pictures of the children's favourite nouns of a category, e.g. favourite mini-beasts, favourite local places, favourite jobs and favourite food.

Word walls

Create eye catching word walls. One flash card equals one brick. Have several bricks to create the word wall with the children. Have blank cards so that the children can write new nouns and add to or make a new word wall shape. They can be used in a variety of ways.

- Common and proper nouns: one wall per noun category, *animals*, *objects*, *names of countries*.

- Making compound nouns.

- Pairs such as single and plural nouns of a noun.

- Word wall for 'an' words and a word wall for 'a' words.

The word ladder

A similar game to 'Consequences'. In groups of four the children are given strips of paper with four sections (see Word ladder template – Teacher resources). The children write a noun on the first section, fold over the paper to hide it and pass it to the next child. They then write another noun on the next and so on. After the strip has been completed, it is opened up and the children read out the four written nouns.

- **Common nouns:** A child writes an example of a person noun, *queen* followed by an animal, place and object. They use the four nouns to orally tell a story.

- **Proper nouns:** Choose four categories in advance and at the end the children use the nouns to tell a story or use the ideas to write a poem.

Word wheel/Word slide

(see Teacher resources for templates)
The teacher or children add nouns to the wheels or slides to explore and discover other words such as plurals with '-s', compound nouns. Also a good reinforcement resource.

Pass the book

The children stand in the circle with a child in the middle with his or her eyes closed. The book is passed round the circle until the child in the middle claps. The child then says a letter of the alphabet. The child holding the book has to say four nouns/proper/plural/compound nouns (the noun subject is decided before the game starts) before the book is passed around the circle and ends up with them again. If the child does not manage to do it, he/she swaps places with the child in the middle.

Matching compound nouns – Fox and geese

Put the children into a circle. Number the children 1 and 2 alternately around the circle. Give all the 1s a beginning noun of a compound noun on a piece of paper. Give all the 2s the second parts of the compound nouns (the cards should be mixed up). Point to a child who is a number 1 and ask them to shout out their noun. A number 2 that has a noun that makes a compound noun calls out their noun. They jump up and try and chase each other around the circle and then sit down.

Other activity ideas

- I'm thinking of a noun. I'm acting a noun. I'm drawing a noun.

- Hangman.

- Team game when noun cards are put in the right category baskets – speed game.

- Word searches – doing them and creating their own.

- Creating fun nonsense compound nouns with drawings.

- Use pictures and colouring books for the children to find nouns/more than one thing – plurals and get them to say or write a list down of what they see.

- Kim's game: Children look at a picture or a tray of objects before it is taken away. They write a list or say what they can remember.

- Highlighting the proper names used on a simple local map.

- Making a list of local shop names and designing their own shop display boards.

- Fun compound nouns with fonts and colours and texts.

- Happy common noun families/Happy proper noun families.

- Matching Bingo – make noun base boards and matching noun cards.

- Trump cards/Fact cards of noun categories.

Common nouns

Learning objectives

- To understand that common nouns name people, creatures, places and objects.

- To identify and use common nouns in sentences.

Resources

- **Lesson** – 'Noun picture cards' (Lesson resources CD-ROM). Copy the noun picture card sheets onto thin card and cut them into individual cards.

- **Group 1 (Year 1)** – Copies of activity sheet 1, 'Green Street Summer Fair' for each child.

- **Group 2 (Year 1/2)** – Copies of activity sheet 2, 'Fun at the Fair' for each child.

- **Group 3 (Year 2)** – Copies of activity sheet 3, 'Panic at the Pet Show' for each child.

Lesson/activity notes

- **Lesson** – Before the lesson, display the noun picture cards around the room.

- **Group 1 (Year 1)** – Children work as a discussion group with adult support.

- **Group 2 (Year 1/2)** – Children working individually on activity sheet and then with a partner or group to play a game.

- **Group 3 (Year 2)** – Children work individually on activity sheet and as pair–share with their work.

Explain to the children that they are going to do common noun activities set round a summer fair. Put the children into their levelled groups and give out the activities. Spend time moving between the groups to discuss individual children's work and assess their level of understanding.

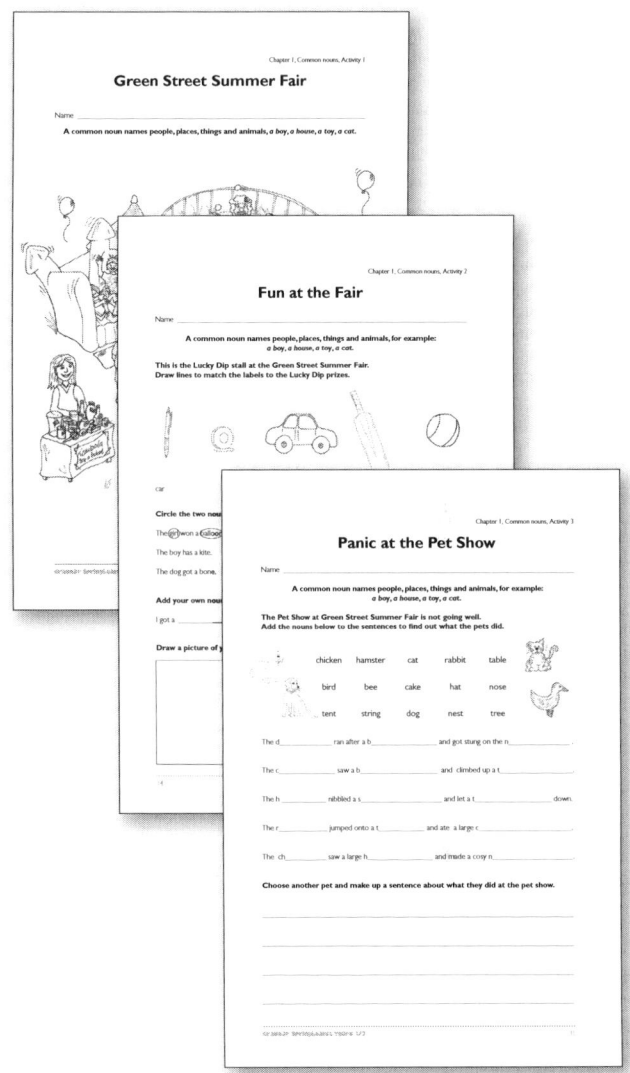

Lesson

Introduction

At the beginning of the lesson, ask the children to look around the room for word and picture cards but not to tell the others what they can see. Explain that they are going to play 'I-spy' using the cards as subjects. Choose one child to start. When the correct answer is given, ask the child to bring up the card and then attach it to a board in front of the class. Once all the cards have been located and displayed, explain that all the words are common nouns.

Main lesson

Highlight that a common noun's job is to name people, creatures, places and objects. Draw four columns on the white board and at the top of each column write: *'People, Animals, Places, Objects'*. With the children, sort the noun cards into the correct columns. Ask the children for a few more common noun examples and add them to the columns. Using a noun from each group, work with the children to write simple sentences. Do the first one as an example, 'The <u>boy</u> fell over.' Underline the noun.

Activities

Group 1 (Year 1)

- Give out the activity sheet 'Green Street Summer Fair' to each child. Remind the children what a common noun is and point to a couple of examples *boy, ball*.

- Then the children look at the picture 'Green Street Summer Fair' to try and find twenty common nouns.

- This can be done as a discussion group with the children taking turns to find and circle a noun on one copy of the picture, or individually with the children finding and circling the nouns on their own copies.

- At the end of the task, look at the chosen nouns. Ask which ones are people, place, object or animal nouns. Record the children's responses as they work.

Group 2 (Year 1/2)

- Give out the activity sheet 'Fun at the Fair' to each child.' If needed, read through the sheet with them.

- Working individually, the children read the labels of five lucky dip prizes and draw lines to link them to their right pictures.

- They then circle two nouns in three sentences, followed by adding a noun word into a sentence about what they would like to get from a lucky dip box. If needed, encourage the children to sound out their noun or look for it as a sight vocabulary.

- Once the children have completed their worksheets, encourage them to play 'I'm thinking of a noun' with a partner or within their group.

Group 3 (Year 2)

- Give out the activity sheet, 'Panic at the Pet Show' to each child within the group.

- Working individually, the children add the missing nouns in the sentences which are joined by 'and'. Before they start, highlight the clues in the sentences to help them, such as the initial letters and the action verbs.

- They then choose a pet of their choice and create a sentence about what the pet may have done at the pet show.

- Encourage the children to share their sentences with each other.

Plenary

Ten minutes before the end of the lesson, bring the children together. Revise what a common noun does. Ask the class questions such as, "What are the four nouns in this sentence? – '*The girl went to the tent to have her face painted like a butterfly.*'" Finish the lesson by encouraging each child to give you a common noun that names a person, a creature, a place and an object.

Support

Encourage those children who are unconfident in identifying common nouns to create their own common noun picture book. The children can draw, cut out pictures from magazines and catalogues or take photos and add them to their noun books under the four categories.

Extension

Encourage the children to collect and write down twenty common nouns of people, places, creatures and objects relating to a given subject or topic, *the sea*, *food*. Ask them to draw a picture and write simple captions for each noun.

Green Street Summer Fair

Name _____

A common noun names people, places, things and animals, *a boy, a house, a toy, a cat.*

Fun at the Fair

Name _____

A common noun names people, places, things and animals, for example:
a boy, a house, a toy, a cat.

This is the Lucky Dip stall at the Green Street Summer Fair.
Draw lines to match the labels to the Lucky Dip prizes.

car   bat   ball   yo-yo   pen

Circle the two nouns in each sentence.

The (girl) won a (balloon).

The boy has a kite.

The dog got a bone.

Add your own noun to this sentence.

I got a _____ from the Lucky Dip box.

Draw a picture of your noun.

Panic at the Pet Show

Name _____

A common noun names people, places, things and animals, for example:
a boy, a house, a toy, a cat.

The Pet Show at Green Street Summer Fair is not going well.
Add the nouns below to the sentences to find out what the pets did.

chicken	hamster	cat	rabbit	table
bird	bee	cake	hat	nose
tent	string	dog	nest	tree

The d_____ ran after a b_____ and got stung on the n_____ .

The c_____ saw a b_____ and climbed up a t_____.

The h _____ nibbled a s_____ and let a t_____ down.

The r_____ jumped onto a t_____ and ate a large c_____.

The ch_____ saw a large h_____ and made a cosy n_____.

Choose another pet and make up a sentence about what they did at the pet show.

_____

_____

_____

_____

Proper nouns

Learning objectives

- To understand that proper nouns give people, places, objects and events their given or special names.

- To learn that proper nouns always begin with a capital letter.

- To understand the difference between a proper noun and a common noun.

Resources

- **Lesson** – Proper noun category headings such as favourite film, favourite day of the week, favourite football club, favourite country, favourite name written on separate pieces of paper. Put one on each table.

- **Group 1 (Year 1)** – Copy and cut up the cards from activity sheet 1 'Proper nouns or Common nouns?' Two tins with 'Proper nouns' labelled in one and 'Common nouns' labelled on the other.

- **Group 2 (Year 1/2)** – Copies of activity sheet 2 'Down at the Shops' for each child.

- **Group 3 (Year 2)** – Copies of activity sheet 3 'Proper noun postcards' for each child. A local map.

Lesson/activity notes

- **Lesson** – This lesson can be adapted from a class to a group exercise by giving each child a heading. Before the lesson put the proper noun headings on each table. Spread the children around the tables in the class.

- **Group 1 (Year 1)** – Working as a discussion group with adult support.

- **Group 2 (Year 1/2)** – Working individually on activity sheet and then as a discussion group.

- **Group 3 (Year 2)** – Work individually on activity sheet and then as a discussion group.

Main lesson

Write the headings on the board and ask each group to tell the class of their choices. Record them under each relevant heading. Once all the groups have given their answers, read through the words under each heading. Explain to the children that all the names are proper nouns. They are the special or given names of people, places, events, and clubs and always start with a capital letter.

Put the children into their levelled groups. Spend time moving between the groups to discuss individual children's work and assess their level of understanding.

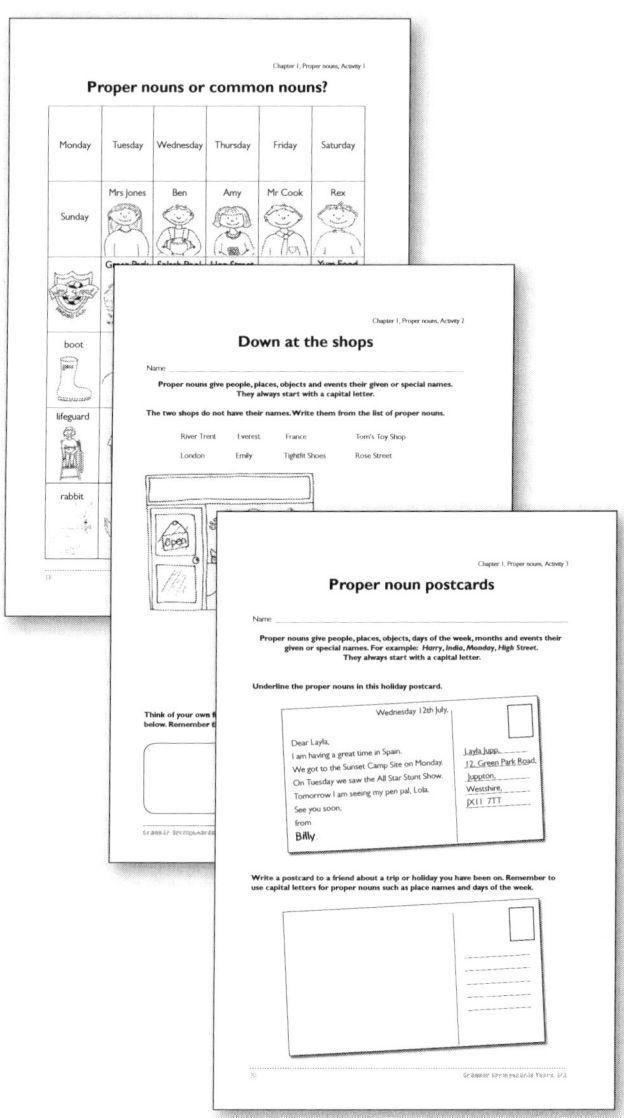

Lesson

Introduction

At the beginning of the lesson, briefly revise examples of common nouns. Explain to the class that they going to learn about another type of noun called a proper noun. Ask each table of children to look at the favourite proper noun subject on the paper and to individually think of their favourite example such as favourite country – India. Encourage them to discuss their reasons briefly with the others in the group.

Activities

Group 1 (Year 1)

- Put the 'Proper nouns' and 'Common nouns' tins and the shuffled pile of 'Proper Nouns or Common Nouns?' cards in front of the children.

- Taking turns, let a child pick up a card and read it out. *Ask 'Should it go in the proper nouns tin or the common nouns tin?'*

- As they make their choice, ask the children their reasons. Record their responses.

- Once the cards are gone, empty the tins and spread out the cards.

- Discuss why the cards in the 'Proper noun' tin are proper nouns. Highlight the capital letters.

- Ask the children for proper noun examples in their local area e.g. shop names, street names.

Group 2 (Year 1/2)

- Give out copies of the activity 2 sheet, 'Down at the Shops', to each child.

- Working individually, the children find the correct proper noun names of two shops from a list of proper nouns and write them under each shop.

- Finally they create their own shop name and draw its shop sign.

- Encourage the children to discuss, in pairs or as a small group, proper noun shop names in their local area. Which ones stand out? Why? Do they all start with capital letters?

Group 3 (Year 2)

- Give out copies of activity sheet 3 'Proper noun postcards' to each child.

- Working individually, the children underline the proper nouns used in a postcard message and its address.

- They then write a postcard message in the postcard frame and an address . Remind them to make sure they add capital letters for their proper nouns. Point to the first postcard as an example.

- Encourage the children to pair-share their postcard messages. Have they added capital letters for all the proper nouns? If time, allow children to draw a picture that could go on the front of their postcard.

Plenary

Before the end of the lesson, bring all the groups together. Revise proper nouns by asking them for the proper noun of a month, a weekday, a car, a name, a football club, a country, a special event or a restaurant. Write the answers on the board and ask the children why they are proper nouns and what should they always begin with.

Support

Encourage the children to collect proper noun examples from different groups to create a display, for example copy out car names such as Honda or Ford from magazines and match them to photos, cut out cereal packet names, collect chocolate bar wrappers. Label each group with the common noun, for example cars, cereals and each item with their proper noun name.

Extension

Ask the children to make proper noun class surveys of different subjects, for example favourite month, favourite films, favourite chocolate. Suggest that they offer a set choice of proper noun names such as favourite author out of choice of five. How would they show their results (for example, graphs)?

Proper nouns or common nouns?

Monday	Tuesday	Wednesday	Thursday	Friday	Saturday
Sunday	Mrs Jones	Ben	Amy	Mr Cook	Rex
	Green Park	Splash Pool	Hop Street		Yum Food Shop
boot	scarf	slide	swing	football	swimmer
lifeguard	house	car	tree	bicycle	cat
rabbit	duck	apple	carrot	bread	milk

Down at the shops

Name _____

Proper nouns give people, places, objects and events their given or special names. They always start with a capital letter.

The two shops do not have their names. Write them from the list of proper nouns.

River Trent   Everest   France   Tom's Toy Shop

London   Emily   Tightfit Shoes   Rose Street

Think of your own fun shop name. Write and draw your fun shop sign in the space below. Remember the capital letters.

Proper noun postcards

Name _____

Proper nouns give people, places, objects, days of the week, months and events their given or special names. For example: *Harry, India, Monday, High Street*. They always start with a capital letter.

Underline the proper nouns in this holiday postcard.

Wednesday 12th July,

Dear Layla,

I am having a great time in Spain.

We got to the Sunset Camp Site on Monday.

On Tuesday we saw the All Star Stunt Show.

Tomorrow I am seeing my pen pal, Lola.

See you soon,

from

Billy.

Layla Jupp,

12, Green Park Road,

Juppton,

Westshire,

JX11 7TT

Write a postcard to a friend about a trip or holiday you have been on. Remember to use capital letters for proper nouns such as place names and days of the week.

Plural noun suffixes '-s' and '-es'

Learning objectives
- To understand that nouns that name more than one thing are called plurals.

- To recognise how some nouns can become plurals by adding '-s' or '-es' on the end.

Resources
- **Lesson** – Two shells, 'A seaside letter' (Lesson resources CD-ROM). Board.

- **Group 1 (Year 1)** – Copies of activity sheet 1 'At the seaside' for each child.

- **Group 2 (Year 1/2)** – Copies of activity sheet 2 'Beachcombing' for each child. Paper and pencils.

- **Group 3 (Year 2)** – Copies of activity sheet 3 'Holiday trips' for each child. Access to books.

Lesson/activity notes
- **Lesson** – Have a whiteboard to show 'A seaside letter' from CD-ROM or show a copy that is large enough for all the children to see.

- **Group 1 (Year 1)** – Children work individually on the activity sheet with adult support.

- **Group 2 (Year 1/2)** – Children work individually on their activity sheets. Work in a small group or pairs to list more plural seaside nouns.

- **Group 3 (Year 2)** – Children work individually on their activity sheet. They pair share their work.

Lesson

Introduction
Hold up one shell. Say to the children, '*I have brought something from the seaside. What is it?*' The children should answer, '*A shell.*' Write the word on the whiteboard. Hold up two shells and ask them what you gave got. They should say '*shells.*' Write the word 'shells' on the board. Ask the children what letter at the end of 'shells' shows that there is more than one. They should answer '-s'. Explain that a noun that names more than one thing is called a plural. Write 'plural' above the word 'shells'.

Main
Explain to the children that you are going to read a letter written about a day at the seaside. Ask the children to listen carefully for plural nouns. When they hear a plural, ask them to put their hand up. Read 'A seaside letter' slowly and take note which children put their hands up

when they hear a plural noun. When you have finished, ask the children to tell you which plural nouns they heard whilst you write them in a column on the board. With the children's help write the singular nouns next to the plurals. Ask the children '*How do these single nouns become plural nouns?*' They should say. '*By adding '-s' at the ends.*'

Write *fox, dress, beach, brush* and underline the x, ss, ch, sh at the end of the word. Explain that with nouns that end in these letters we add '-es' to their ends to make them plural. Write the '-es' to the verbs. Ask the children to think of a few more nouns with same endings such as *box, princess,* etc.

Put the children into their levelled groups. Spend time moving between the groups to discuss individual children's work and assess their level of understanding.

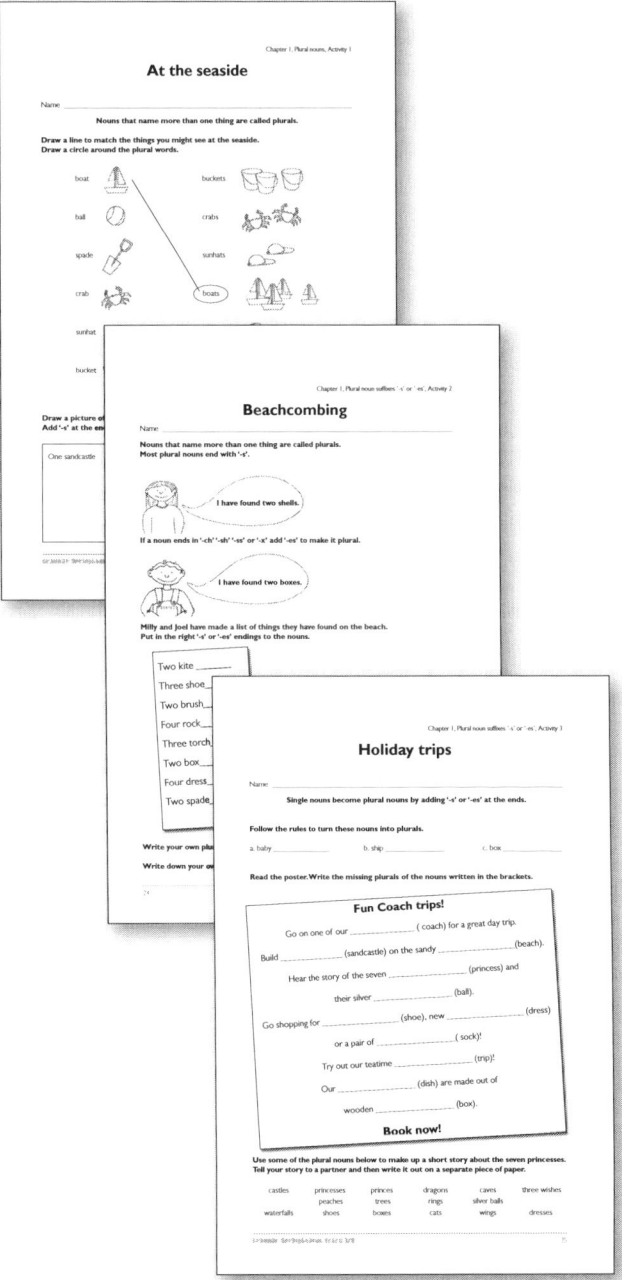

Activities

Group 1 (Year 1)

- Give out the copies of activity sheet 1 'At the seaside' to each of the children.

- The adult support or teacher reads the instructions with the children.

- Working individually, the children match the singular nouns with their plural forms by drawing lines to connect the two.

- They then put a circle around the plural nouns. Ask the children to point to the '-s' at the end of the plural nouns.

- The children then draw a picture of one sandcastle and a picture of two sandcastles.

- At the end of the activity, take note whether the children independently add '-s' to 'sandcastle' to make it a plural noun.

Group 2 (Year 1/2)

- Give out the copies of the activity sheet 2, 'Beachcombing' to the children. Read the activity sheet, pointing to the speech bubble plural rules.

- Working individually, the children add '-s' or '-es' to the list of objects found on a beach.

- They then write their own plural noun ending with '-s' and a plural noun ending in '-es'.

- If time, ask the children to work together in pairs to list more seaside beachcombing plurals ending in '-s' or '-es'.

Group 3 (Year 2)

- Give out copies of activity sheet 3, 'Holiday trips', to the children. Explain that it is a poster advertising holiday day trips by coach. Read through the plural rules including replacing '-y' with '-i' for nouns ending with '-y'.

- Working individually, the children rewrite three singular nouns into plurals.

- They then write the missing plurals from the singular nouns in brackets to complete the poster. Get children to discuss why some plurals end in '-s' and some in '-es'.

- Finally, the children should work, individually or in pairs, to write a short traditional story using the plurals given in a word box. Let the children read out their story to others.

Plenary

Before the end of the lesson, bring all the groups together. Draw a face on the board and write the word 'face' above it. Ask the children *'What is a noun that names more than one thing or person?'* They should say *'plural'*. Draw another face next to the other one and ask *'What letter do I add to turn 'face' into 'faces?'* They should say *'s'*. Draw a big smile on the faces.

Support

To reinforce the idea of plural nouns ending with '-s' and '-es', play simple games using plural and single noun flash cards. For example, shuffle out singular and plural noun cards together and lay them out for the children to put into pairs.

Extension

Highlight that some single nouns can also be plurals, such as *sand*, *fish*, *gold*, and *sheep*. Ask the children to research similar noun plurals, *deer*, *pants*, *trousers*, *seaweed*. Put a list up on a display area or create a poster for the children to add to when they come across these plural nouns.

At the seaside

Name _____

Nouns that name more than one thing are called plurals.

Draw a line to match the things you might see at the seaside.
Draw a circle around the plural words.

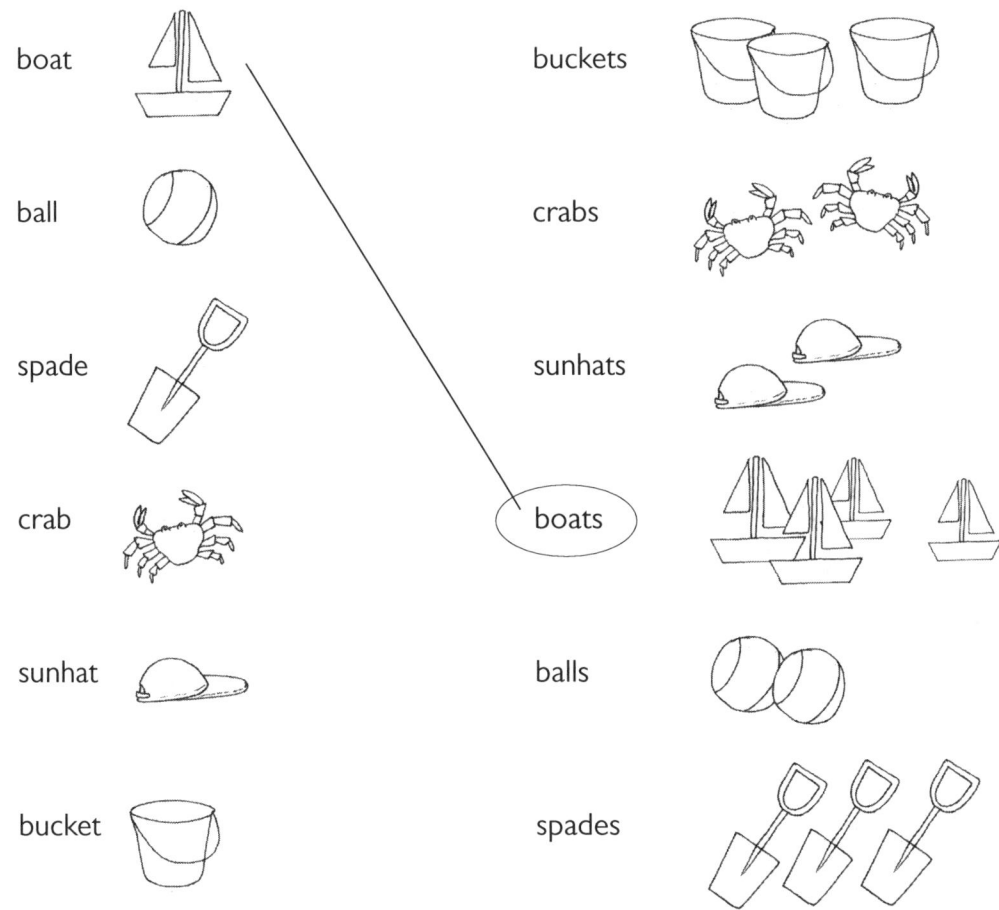

boat		buckets	
ball		crabs	
spade		sunhats	
crab		boats	
sunhat		balls	
bucket		spades	

Draw a picture of one sandcastle in the first box and two sandcastles in the second box. Add '-s' at the end of the word to make it a plural.

| One sandcastle | Two sandcastle _ |
| | |

Beachcombing

Name _____

Nouns that name more than one thing are called plurals.
Most plural nouns end with '-s'.

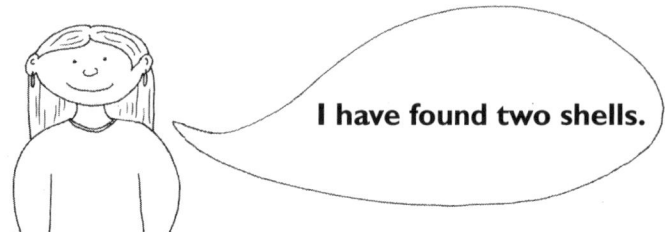

I have found two shells.

If a noun ends in '-ch' '-sh' '-ss' or '-x' add '-es' to make it plural.

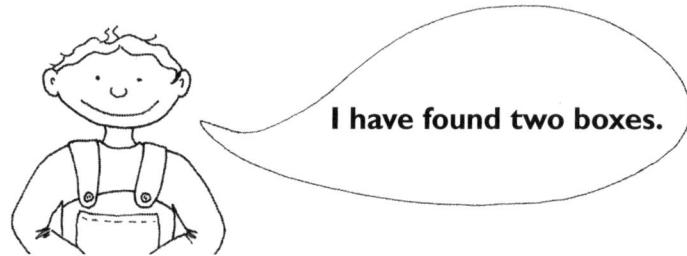

I have found two boxes.

Milly and Joel have made a list of things they have found on the beach.
Put in the right '-s' or '-es' endings to the nouns.

Two kite _____

Three shoe_____

Two brush_____

Four rock_____

Three torch_____

Two box_____

Four dress_____

Two spade_____

Write your own plural noun ending with '-s.' _____

Write down your own plural noun ending with '-es' _____

Holiday trips

Name _____

Single nouns become plural nouns by adding '-s' or '-es' at the ends.

Follow the rules to turn these nouns into plurals.

a. baby _____   b. ship _____   c. box _____

Read the poster. Write the missing plurals of the nouns written in the brackets.

Fun Coach trips!

Go on one of our _____ (coach) for a great day trip.

Build _____ (sandcastle) on the sandy _____(beach).

Hear the story of the seven _____ (princess) and

their silver _____ (ball).

Go shopping for _____ (shoe), new _____ (dress)

or a pair of _____(sock)!

Try out our teatime _____ (trip)!

Our _____ (dish) are made out of

wooden _____ (box).

Book now!

Use some of the plural nouns below to make up a short story about the seven princesses. Tell your story to a partner and then write it out on a separate piece of paper.

castles	princesses	princes	dragons	caves	three wishes
	peaches	trees	rings	silver balls	
waterfalls	shoes	boxes	cats	wings	dresses

Compound nouns

Learning objectives
* To understand that a compound noun is made of two nouns.

* To identify and use compound nouns.

Resources
* **Lesson** – 'Compound noun sheet 1' and 'Compound noun sheet 2' (Lesson resources CD-ROM). Copy and cut up the sheets into individual cards.

* **Group 1 (Year 1)** – 'Professor Compound's noun machine' (Lesson resources instructions on CD-ROM) Activity sheets 1, 'Compound noun picture cards 1' and 'Compound noun pictures cards 2'. Activity sheets per pair or group.

* **Group 2 (Year 1/2)** – 'Compound noun-maker template' and 'Compound noun slide strips', for each pair of children and copies onto card of 'Word slide strips' (Lesson resources CD-ROM). Paper and pencils, Copy and cut out the compound noun maker/strips.

* **Group 3 (Year 2)** – 'Professor Compound's card game' (Lesson resources CD-ROM.) Make up the cards before the lesson.

Lesson/activity notes
* **Lesson** – Before the lesson, set out the 'Compound noun sheet 2' on tables around the classroom. Keep the 'Compound noun sheet 1' with you. If possible start the lesson away from the class tables.

* **Group 1 (Year 1)** – Children work as a small discussion group with adult support.

* **Group 2 (Year 1/2)** – Children working in pairs and then share with another pair. Need adult/teacher support.

* **Group 3 (Year 2)** – Children work as one group or groups of three or more to play a card game.

nouns beginning with 'door' and write them by the door shape, e.g. doorknob, doorbell, doorman.

Main lesson
Put the children into mixed pairs. Give each pair a card from 'Compound noun sheet 1'. Explain that they need to search the tables for a second noun card to make a compound noun. Show two cards as an example e.g. 'hair' 'brush'. Once they have made their compound noun, they must think of a sentence they can use it in. Ask each pair of children to show and read out their compound noun and say their sentence.

Explain to the children that they are going to work on compound noun activities. Put the children into their levelled groups and give out the activities. Spend time moving between the groups to discuss individual children's work and assess their level of understanding.

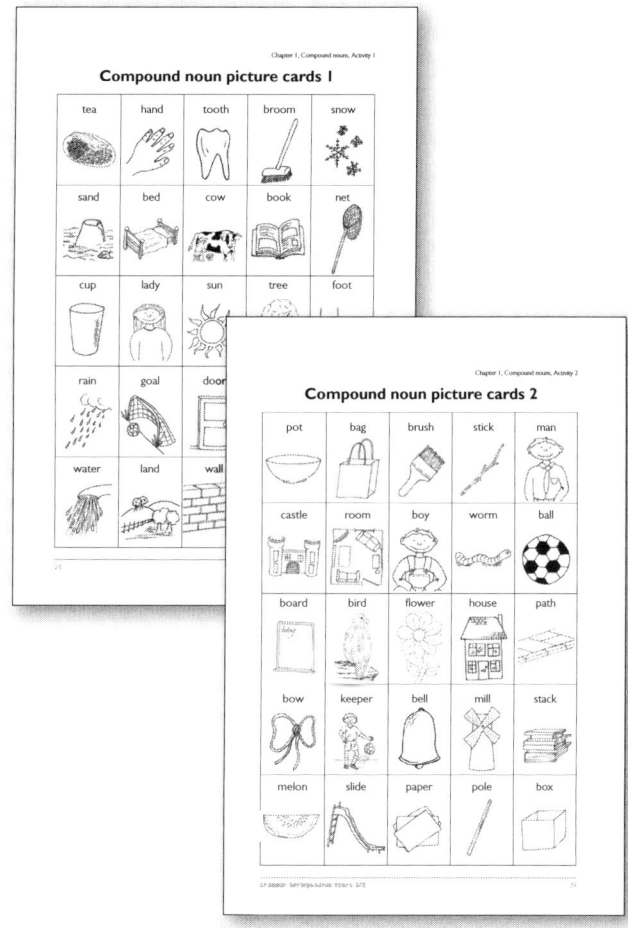

Lesson

Introduction
Draw a large door on the white board and write 'door' in the middle. Explain to the children that they are going to help you think of words that start with the word 'door'. Start off with 'doorstep'. Highlight how the word is made from the two nouns, 'door' and 'step'. Explain that words made up from two words are called compound nouns. Encourage the children to think of a few more compound

Activities

Group 1 (Year 1)
* Put 'Professor Compound's noun machine' in front of the children with the first set of picture compound noun cards in a pile and the second set laid out picture up on the table.

* Ask a child to feed a card from pile one through the machine. Ask the child what the picture noun is.

- Ask them to find a picture noun from the laid out cards that could be added at the end of the first picture noun to make a compound noun, *teapot*.

- Write out the compound noun on paper and put it by the two cards.

- Let the children take turns until all the compound nouns are found. Can they make any more compound nouns from the cards, *teabag*?

Group 2 (Year 1/2)
- Give out the 'Compound noun maker,' several 'Compound noun slide strips' and a blank piece of paper to each pair of children.

- Ask the children to make a list of eight compound nouns.

- When they have made their list, ask them to write the first nouns on one word slide strip and the second nouns on the other.

- Let them attach the two strips into their 'Compound noun maker' and then swap it with another pair.

- Ask the children to use the swapped 'Compound noun maker' to find compound nouns and write simple sentences with them.

Group 3 (Year 2)
- Shuffle the set of 'Professor Compound's card game' cards and deal them all out to the children.

- The children look at their cards for compound word matches and then place them face up on the table.

- One child starts by choosing a card from the child to their left. If it matches one of their cards they put the pair down. If not, it stays in their hand.

- The game continues with the next child picking a card from the left.

- The game ends when one child is left with the 'Professor Compound card'.

- Ask the children in turn what their compound nouns mean and to make sentences using them.

Plenary
Before the end of the lesson, bring all the groups together. Ask the children for different examples of a compound noun. Ask what a compound noun is made of 'two nouns'. If time, have fun and create nonsense compound nouns, for example *socksausage*.

Support
Encourage the children to create and draw three of their own compound noun picture cards for 'Professor Compound's word machine' game. They can see if another child or children can make the compound nouns and vice versa.

Extension
Highlight that some words such as 'moonlight' or 'handstand 'are made up of a noun and verb. These are called compound words. Encourage the children to make small books of compound nouns and compound words with comic style illustrations and the nouns and verbs written underneath.

Compound noun picture cards 1

tea	hand	tooth	broom	snow
sand	bed	cow	book	net
cup	lady	sun	tree	foot
rain	goal	door	wind	hay
water	land	wall	flag	letter

Compound noun picture cards 2

pot	bag	brush	stick	man
castle	room	boy	worm	ball
board	bird	flower	house	path
bow	keeper	bell	mill	stack
melon	slide	paper	pole	box

Making nouns with suffixes

Learning objectives

- To change verbs into nouns by adding the suffix '-er'.

- To make new nouns by adding the suffixes '-ness' and '-ment'.

Resources

- **Lesson** – Board or large paper with pen.

- **Group 1 (Year 1)** – Copies of activity sheet 1, 'Who is doing the actions?' for each child.

- **Group 2 (Year 1/2)** – Copies of activity sheet 2, 'Making new nouns with '-ness' and '-ment'' for each child. Scissors, paper.

- **Group 3 (Year 2)** – Copies of activity sheet 3, 'Glossary of nouns with '-ness' and '-ment' for each child. Children's dictionary.

Lesson/activity notes

- **Lesson** – Work as a discussion group.

- **Group 1 (Year 1)** – Children work as a group for discussion and individually on the activity with adult support.

- **Group 2 (Year 1/2)** – Children work in pairs or within a group.

- **Group 3 (Year 2)** – Children work in pairs or individually, depending on ability.

Lesson

Introduction

Write out these words in a vertical list on a board or on a large sheet of paper, if sitting at a table with children: *sing, dance, build*. Remind the children that they are verbs. Under the verbs, write two more lists of the following words: *pay, move, agree* and *bald, forgive, happy*. Highlight the verbs and adjectives in these lists. Announce that you are going to turn all these verbs and adjectives into nouns by adding on small sets of letters. Explain that these are called suffixes.

Main lesson

Write the suffixes ' -er', '-ness' and '-ment' for the children to see. Say the sounds for each suffix and let them say the sounds after you. Explain that you are going to add the suffix '-er' to the end of one of the words in the first list - sing- singer. Discuss how the verb becomes the noun of the person who does that action. Let children take turns to add '-er' to the other verbs.

Continue along the same line with the other lists of words. Add the suffix '-ment' to the second list and discuss the noun meanings and then the suffix '-ness' to the third list. Highlight the '-i' for '-y' rule for the word 'happy'.

Explain to the children that in their activities they are going to make more nouns using suffixes '-er', '-ness' or '-ment'.

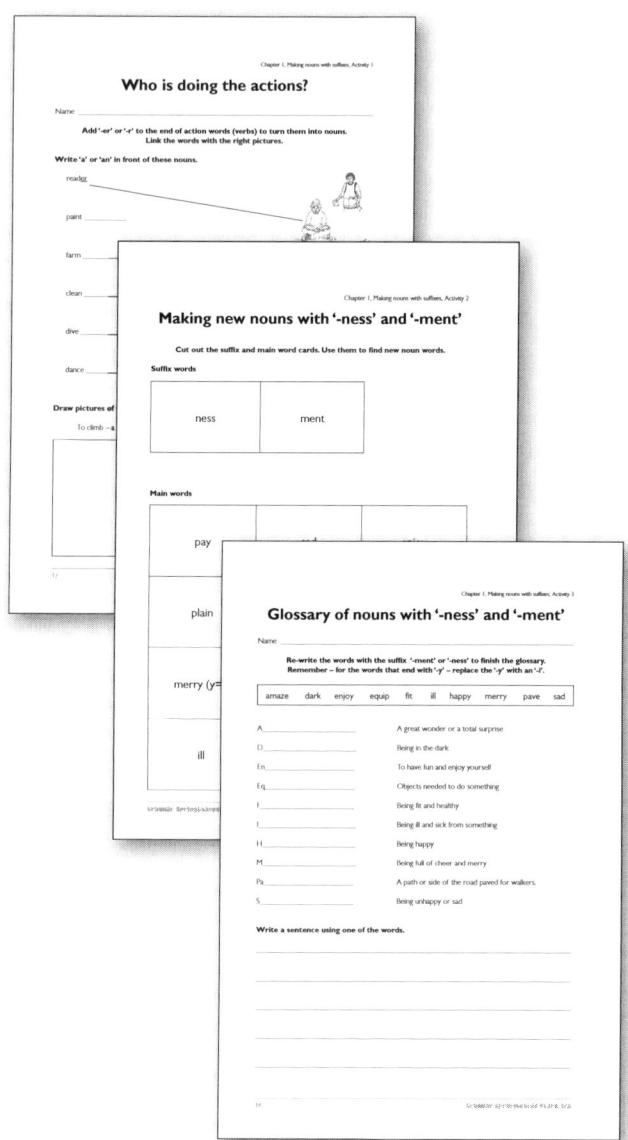

Activities

Group 1 (Year 1)

- Give out the copies of 'Who is doing the actions?' to each child.

- Read the verbs down the left hand side of the page. Discuss how the verbs can be turned into nouns by adding '-er' and '-r'. Highlight how the nouns describe the person who does the verb actions.

- Working individually, the children add '-er' or '-r' to the verbs and then draw lines to match the nouns to the right pictures.

- The children then draw pictures of a climber and a baker. Discuss when to add '-r' to the end of verbs - when the verb ends in 'e'.

- Encourage the children to suggest other names that have '-er' or '-r'.

Group 2 (Year 1/2)
- Give out the copies of 'Making new nouns with '-ness' and '-ment'' for each child.

- Either let the children cut out the suffix words and main words or cut them out for them.

- In pairs or working individually, let the children use the cards to investigate making nouns with the suffixes. Discuss the rule for root words that end with '-y'.

- Encourage children to orally make sentences using the suffixes and then write them out to share with others.

Group 3 (Year 2)
- Give out the copies of 'Glossary of nouns with '-ness' and '-ment'' for each child.

- Discuss with the children what a Glossary is and how it can be used.

- Working in pairs or individually, the children rewrite the words at the top of the sheet and change them into nouns by adding the right suffix.

- Give the children access to a children's dictionary as support.

Plenary
Ten minutes before the end of the lesson, bring all the children together to share their work. Discuss what a suffix is and the spelling rules related to some of the words. Highlight how the adjectives make their writing more interesting.

Extension
Ask the children to write out their suffix noun words on separate cards so that they can be displayed on a board next to the original verb or adjective words.

Who is doing the actions?

Name _____

Add '-er' or '-r' to the end of action words (verbs) to turn them into nouns.
Link the words with the right pictures.

Write 'a' or 'an' in front of these nouns.

reader

paint _____

farm _____

clean _____

dive _____

dance _____

Draw pictures of these nouns which end in '-er'.

To climb – a climber

To bake – a baker

Making new nouns with '-ness' and '-ment'

Cut out the suffix and main word cards. Use them to find new noun words.

Suffix words

ness	ment

Main words

pay	sad	enjoy
plain	pave	amaze
merry (y=i)	equip	happy (y=i)
ill	dark	fitness

Glossary of nouns with '-ness' and '-ment'

Name _____

Re-write the words with the suffix '-ment' or '-ness' to finish the glossary.
Remember – for the words that end with '-y' – replace the '-y' with an '-i'.

| amaze | dark | enjoy | equip | fit | ill | happy | merry | pave | sad |

A_____   A great wonder or a total surprise

D_____   Being in the dark

En_____   To have fun and enjoy yourself

Eq_____   Objects needed to do something

F_____   Being fit and healthy

I_____   Being ill and sick from something

H_____   Being happy

M_____   Being full of cheer and merry

Pa_____   A path or side of the road paved for walkers.

S_____   Being unhappy or sad

Write a sentence using one of the words.

_____

_____

_____

_____

_____

Expanded noun phrases

Learning objectives
- To understand what a noun phrase is.

- To create simple expanded noun phrases for description and specification.

Resources
- **Lesson** – Board or large paper with pen.

- **Group 1 (Year 1)** – Copies of activity sheet 1, 'Labelled picture of a giraffe' for each child. Ruler.

- **Group 2 (Year 1/2)** – Copies of activity sheet 2, 'Making expanded noun phrases' for pairs of children. Colouring pencils.

- **Group 3 (Year 2)** – Copies of activity sheet 3, 'Using expanded noun phrases' for each child. Pencils and colouring pencils.

Lesson/activity notes
- **Lesson** – Within the lesson, the children are split into two groups and work within those groups with a partner. If working with a pair of children, they can do the different group activity.

- **Group 1 (Year 1)** – Children work as a group for discussion and individually on the activity with adult support.

- **Group 2 (Year 1/2)** – Children work in pairs.

- **Group 3 (Year 2)** – Children work in pairs or individually, depending on ability.

Lesson

Introduction
On the board or on a piece of paper, write 'There is a rabbit.' Ask the children what the noun is in the simple sentence. Explain to the children that the sentence doesn't tell us anything about the rabbit or what it is doing or where it is. Write 'There is a large brown rabbit jumping into a dark hole'. Discuss how by adding extra information about the rabbit (noun) readers can build pictures in their minds.

Main lesson
Explain that adding extra words to a main noun is called a noun phrase. Underline the phrase before 'rabbit' and read it out – 'There is a large brown'. Ask the children what type of words are used to describe the rabbit (adjectives).

Now underline the noun phrase after the main noun and read it out – 'jumping into a dark hole.' Highlight the use of

a verb to show what the rabbit is doing and then highlight 'dark hole' which shows where it is going.

Split the children into two groups. Within each group, ask the children to work with a partner. Ask the first group to think in their pairs of different front noun phrases to describe the rabbit and ask the second group in pairs to think of different behind noun phrases of what the rabbit was doing, or where it was going. After several minutes, have fun with the groups creating new noun phrases for the rabbit.

Explain to the children that they are going to work on creating noun phrases in a set of activities.

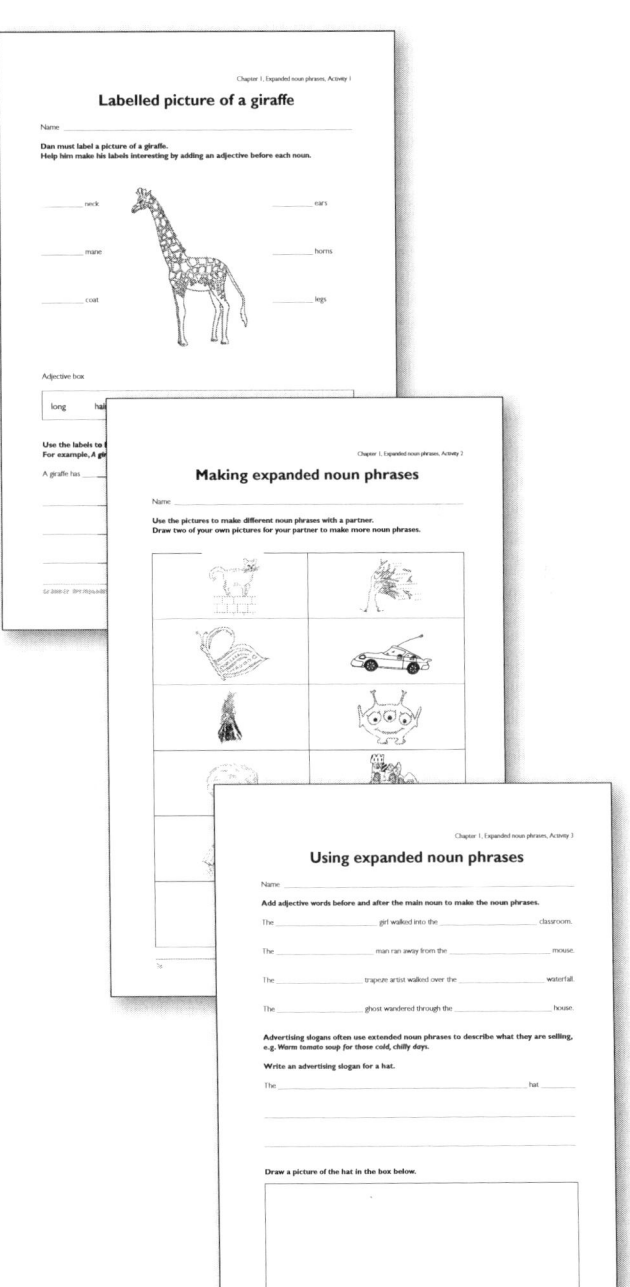

Activities

Group 1 (Year 1)

- Give out the copies of 'Labelled picture of a giraffe' to each child.

- Children work individually to choose the right adjective from a list of adjectives to place in front of nouns for labels of a giraffe. Encourage the children to discuss what each adjective is describing such as numbers, size, texture, etc.

- The children then use the labels to write a sentence describing the giraffe. Let the children share their sentences and discuss how an adjective added in front of a noun allows us to know what the noun is like.

Group 2 (Year 1/2)

- Give out the copies of 'Making expanded noun phrases' to each pair of children.

- Read out the instructions at the top of the sheet. Remind the children what a noun phrase is and if needed choose the first picture to do an example of a noun phrase.

- Working in pairs, let the children decide what the main noun is in each picture and let them explore ways to describe it as a phrase to go before the noun, for example: 'the fat, smiley cat'.

- Let them share their noun phrases with other pairs. Challenge them to expand the phrases even further by adding a phrase after the main noun and describing where it is, – 'the fat, smiley cat sat on the wall'.

- The children then create two of their own noun phrase pictures to make more noun phrases.

- Let the pairs share their noun phrases with others. How do they all differ?

Group 3 (Year 2)

- Give out the copies of 'Using expanded noun phrases' to each child. Remind the children what a noun phrase is and why it is used.

- Working individually, the children add their own choice of adjectives before a main noun to describe it and another adjective to describe where the main noun is.

- They then write an advertising slogan for a hat using an expanded noun phrase and using the example on the sheet as guidance. They complete this by drawing their hat.

- Once the activity is completed, let the children share their noun phrase slogans.

Plenary

Ten minutes before the end of the lesson, bring all the children together. Let them share their expanded noun phrases with the rest of the class or groups. Have fun discussing the examples and highlight the use of verbs, adjectives, prepositions and other nouns in the sentences. Discuss why noun phrases can make writing more interesting.

Support

Focus on the front noun phrase. Give the children a choice of main noun ideas and adjectives, verbs and other nouns to help them create a noun phrase.

Extension

Let children look in fiction books for examples of noun phrases. Highlight a sentence and ask the children to find the main noun and the phrases.

Labelled picture of a giraffe

Name _____

Dan must label a picture of a giraffe.
Help him make his labels interesting by adding an adjective before each noun.

_____ neck

_____ mane

_____ coat

_____ ears

_____ horns

_____ legs

Adjective box

long	hairy	spotty	brown	small	thin	one	two	four

Use the labels to help you write a caption about the giraffe.
For example, *A giraffe has four thin legs and is very tall.*

A giraffe has _____

_____

_____

_____

Making expanded noun phrases

Name _____

Use the pictures to make different noun phrases with a partner.
Draw two of your own pictures for your partner to make more noun phrases.

Using expanded noun phrases

Name _____

Add adjective words before and after the main noun to make the noun phrases.

The _____ girl walked into the _____ classroom.

The _____ man ran away from the _____ mouse.

The _____ trapeze artist walked over the _____ waterfall.

The _____ ghost wandered through the _____ house.

Advertising slogans often use extended noun phrases to describe what they are selling, e.g. *Warm tomato soup for those cold, chilly days.*

Write an advertising slogan for a hat.

The _____ hat _____

_____

_____

Draw a picture of the hat in the box below.

Chapter 2 – Pronouns
Pronoun information

Pronoun	A word that can replace a noun or noun phrase to make a text flow and cut down on repetition.	*Ali ran to the park. Ali went on the swings.'* becomes *'Ali ran to the park. He went on the swings.'*
Personal pronouns	Words that replace names of people, places, objects and creatures.	
	Subject personal pronouns: I, you, she, he, we, it and they. These pronouns replace the names of people or objects that do actions.	*'Josh kicked the ball.'* becomes *'He kicked the ball'.*
	Object personal pronouns: me, you, her, him, it, us and them. These pronouns replace the names of the people or things that are affected by an action.	*'Kim hugged Gran.'* becomes *'Kim hugged her.'*
Singular pronouns	Words that replace single nouns such as one person or one object. I, my, me, mine, you, your, yours, she, her, hers, he, him, his, it, its.	*'Mrs King read Harry's letter.'* becomes *'She read his letter.'* *'The snake hissed. The snake was cross.'* becomes *'The snake hissed. It was cross.'*
Plural pronouns	Words that replace plural nouns such as more than one person or object. We, us, our, ours, you, your, yours, they, them, their, theirs.	*'Tim let the fish go.'* becomes *'Tim let them go.'*
Interrogative pronouns	Question words that replace a person or objects that is being asked about. Who? Whose? Which? What? Whom?	*Who is the boss? What is his address? Whose shoes are these?*
Demonstrative pronouns	Words that replace singular or plural nouns and highlight the location of an object. This, that, these, those.	*'You get these crisps and I'll get the crisps over there.'* becomes *'You get these crisps and I'll get those.'*
Possessive pronouns	Words that are used to replace a noun to show ownership. Mine, his, hers, its, yours, ours, theirs.	*'This is Sara's book and this is your book.'* becomes *'This is Sara's book and this is yours.'*

Pronoun objective chart

Objectives and year group	Singular pronouns	Plural pronouns
Word – Year 1		
Recognise nouns.	★	★
Recognise pronouns.	★	★
Recognise singular and plural pronouns.	★	★
Word – Year 2		
Use nouns.	★	★
Use pronouns.	★	★
Use singular and plural pronouns.	★	★
Sentence – Year 1		
How words can combine to make sentences.	★	★
Sentence – Year 2		
Different sentences statement, question, exclamation, command.	★	★
Text – Year 1		
Sequencing sentences to form short narrative – orally.	★	★
Text – Year 2		
Use of present and past tense in writing.	★	★
Punctuation – Year 1		
Capital letters, full stops, question marks, exclamation marks to demarcate sentences.	★	★
Capital letters for names and for the personal pronoun 'I'.	★	★
Punctuation – Year 2		
Capital letters, full stops, question marks, exclamation marks to demarcate sentences.	★	★

Pronoun springboards

Pronoun word wall

Create a pronoun word wall. Walls could include a singular pronoun wall, plural pronoun wall and simple sentences wall with the pronoun cards in a different colour.

Pronoun sentence display

Have pronoun flash cards on a display board with other words so that the children can use them to make up simple sentences when they are asked, or voluntarily in a quiet time.

The missing pronouns

Have a pronoun challenge. Have a sentence on the display board and say that someone has taken the pronouns out. Ask the children if they could add them back in. Change the sentences over the week and get the children to watch out and add in the missing pronouns.

Pronoun songs and rhymes

Let the children listen to or read a poem a nursery rhyme or a simple song, 'Sing a song of sixpence'. Ask the children to make a mark on a piece of paper every time they hear a pronoun. You could also do this with short stories.

A pronoun rug

Draw a big patchwork rug on paper. Put a variety of pronouns in some of the shapes and then fill the rest of the shapes with nouns, verbs, adjectives etc. Ask the children to colour in all the pronouns in one colour and the other words in another colour. You could ask more able children to colour nouns in one colour and verbs in another.

Adding pronouns

1. Copy a simple text from a picture book or short story onto the computer and ask the children to delete the personal nouns such as names and type in personal pronouns. Discuss the difference.

2. Make copies of a story text or poem relating to the child's ability. Give a child or a small group of children a copy of the text and ask them to cut out all the pronouns in the text. Ask them to sort out the pronouns that are masculine, feminine and relating to a person. Give them another text with the pronouns blanked out and ask them to replace them with their cut out pronouns.

The word ladder

A similar game to 'Consequences'. In groups of four the children are given strips of paper with four sections (see Word ladder Template – Teacher resources CD-ROM). The children write a pronoun on the first section, fold over the paper to hide it and pass it to the next child. They then write another pronoun on the next and so on. After the strip has been completed it is opened up and the children read out the four written pronouns.

They use the pronouns to orally tell a short story or a recount. They could also use them to write a short story or poem.

Singular pronouns

Learning objectives
- To understand that a pronoun is a word that takes the place of a noun.

- To recognise and use singular pronouns.

Resources
- **Lesson** – 'Little Miss Muffet' and 'Singular pronoun cards 1' (Lesson resources CD-ROM).

- **Group 1 (Year 1)** – Scissors, glue, copies of activity sheet 1, 'Little Red Riding Hood' for each child.

- **Group 2 (Year 1/2)** – Copies of activity sheet 2 'Pronoun Tales' for each child. Singular Pronoun word search (Teacher resources CD-ROM)

- **Group 3 (Year 2)** – Copies of activity sheet 3, 'The Gingerbread Man' for each child.

Lesson/activity notes
- **Lesson** – Have the pronoun cards on display as the children work on their activities.

- **Group 1 (Year 1)** – Children can work individually or in a group on their activity sheets. The group will need adult support.

- **Group 2 (Year 1/2)** – Children work individually on their activity sheet and their word search.

- **Group 3 (Year 2)** – Children work individually on their activity sheet and then discuss their work in pairs.

Lesson

Introduction
Display 'Little Miss Muffet', for all the children to see. Read the original rhyme with the children. Point to version 2 and read it out slowly. Ask the children what is different about this version. Some of the children may say *'There are lots of Miss Muffets'* or *'Miss Muffet' is used instead of the word 'her.'* Ask the children which version sounds better. Why? Underline the word 'her' in the original version. Explain that 'her' is a word called a pronoun which takes the place of a noun to make a sentence sound better

Main lesson
Ask some children to come out and hold up the 'Singular pronoun cards'. Explain that all these words are pronouns and are used to replace single nouns, for example one person or an object. Make up a sentence without a pronoun such as 'Grace loves Grace's rabbit'. Ask the children which pronoun could be used instead of Grace

and write the sentence on the board: 'Grace loves her rabbit' or 'She loves her rabbit'. Once a pronoun is used, put the card down. With the children make up more sentences until all the pronouns are used.

Explain to the children that they are going to do activities with pronouns. Put the children into their levelled groups. Spend time moving between the groups to discuss individual children's work and assess their level of understanding.

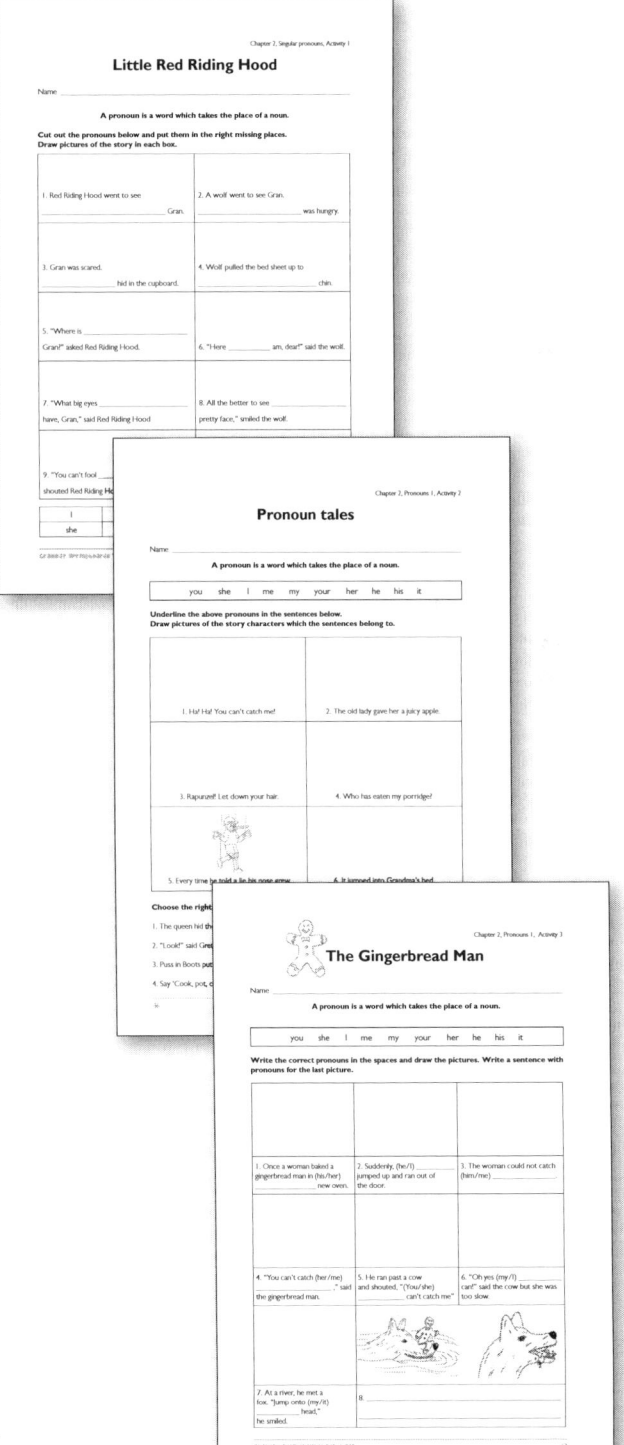

Activities

Group 1 (Year 1)

- Give out the copies of activity sheet, 'Little Red Riding Hood' to each of the children.

- Ask the children to cut out the pronouns from the bottom of the page and read them out.

- Go through the story with the children.

- Go back to the first frame and read through the first sentence. Ask them to choose a pronoun to put in the missing space.

- Ask them to read out the sentence. Does it make sense? If it does, let them stick the pronoun into the space.

- Once the story is complete, let the children take turns to read out the story. Let them draw the pictures.

Group 2 (Year 1/2)

- Give out copies of the activity sheet 'Pronoun Tales' to the children.

- Working individually, the children underline pronouns in sentences and draw matching story characters.

- Finally they choose the right pronoun for four sentences.

- If time, give the children the singular pronoun word search.

Group 3 (Year 2)

- Give out copies of the activity sheet 'The Gingerbread Man' to the children.

- Working individually the children must write the correct pronoun to the sentences of a traditional story.

- They then write the last two sentences with pronouns and illustrate the comic strip.

- Once they have completed the activity, ask them to work in pairs and discuss which nouns the pronouns could have replaced. Which text works better? Why?

Plenary

Before the end of the lesson, bring all the groups together. Ask *'How do you think pronouns make sentences in writing and speaking sound better?'* Encourage them to look at stories and rhymes to see how many pronouns they can spot.

Support

Choose a story or a nursery rhyme with a simple text and read the story with the children. Point to singular pronouns within the different sentences. With the children add the noun that the pronoun replaced and compare the two sentences.

Extension

Highlight that singular pronouns are words that replace single nouns such as one person or one object. Let the children listen to the lyrics of a song. Ask them to make a tally of how many times they hear a singular pronoun. Give them a copy of the lyrics to highlight and check against their pronoun tally.

Little Red Riding Hood

Name _____

A pronoun is a word which takes the place of a noun.

**Cut out the pronouns below and put them in the right missing places.
Draw pictures of the story in each box.**

1. Red Riding Hood went to see _____ Gran.	2. A wolf went to see Gran. _____ was hungry.
3. Gran was scared. _____ hid in the cupboard.	4. Wolf pulled the bed sheet up to _____ chin.
5. "Where is _____ Gran?" asked Red Riding Hood.	6. "Here _____ am, dear!" said the wolf.
7. "What big eyes _____ have, Gran," said Red Riding Hood	8. All the better to see _____ pretty face," smiled the wolf.
9. "You can't fool _____!" shouted Red Riding Hood.	10. She chased _____ into the woods.

I	me	my	you	your
she	her	he	him	his

Pronoun tales

Name _____

A pronoun is a word which takes the place of a noun.

you	she	I	me	my	your	her	he	his	it

Underline the above pronouns in the sentences below.
Draw pictures of the story characters which the sentences belong to.

1. Ha! Ha! You can't catch me!	2. The old lady gave her a juicy apple.
3. Rapunzel! Let down your hair.	4. Who has eaten my porridge?
5. Every time <u>he</u> told a lie <u>his</u> nose grew.	6. It jumped into Grandma's bed.

Choose the right pronouns in the brackets and write them in the spaces.

1. The queen hid the pea. The princess did not know _____ (I/it) was there.

2. "Look!" said Gretel. "_____ (My/Her) house is made from sweets."

3. Puss in Boots put the rabbit in the sack. _____ (He/His) gave it to the King.

4. Say 'Cook, pot, cook'. It will give _____ (it/you) hot porridge.

The Gingerbread Man

Name _____

A pronoun is a word which takes the place of a noun.

you she I me my your her he his it

Write the correct pronouns in the spaces and draw the pictures. Write a sentence with pronouns for the last picture.

<table>
<tr><td></td><td></td><td></td></tr>
<tr>
<td>1. Once a woman baked a gingerbread man in (his/her) _____ new oven.</td>
<td>2. Suddenly, (he/I) _____ jumped up and ran out of the door.</td>
<td>3. The woman could not catch (him/me) _____ .</td>
</tr>
<tr><td></td><td></td><td></td></tr>
<tr>
<td>4. "You can't catch (her/me) _____ ," said the gingerbread man.</td>
<td>5. He ran past a cow and shouted, "(You/she) _____ can't catch me"</td>
<td>6. "Oh yes (my/I) _____ can!" said the cow but she was too slow.</td>
</tr>
<tr><td></td><td colspan="2"></td></tr>
<tr>
<td>7. At a river, he met a fox. "Jump onto (my/it) _____ head," he smiled.</td>
<td colspan="2">8. _____

_____</td>
</tr>
</table>

Plural pronouns

Learning objectives

- To understand that a pronoun is a word that takes the place of a noun.

- To recognise and use plural pronouns.

Resources

- **Lesson** – 'Three Blind Mice' and 'Plural pronoun cards' (Lesson resources CD-ROM).

- **Group 1 (Year 1)** – A set of 'Plural pronoun cards', a set of activity sheet 1 'Noun space cards', paper and pen or whiteboard for all the group.

- **Group 2 (Year 1/2)** – Copies of activity sheet 2.1, 'Pronoun blast off' for each child and activity sheet 2.2. 'Pronoun Blast Off 2' to each pair of children.

- **Group 3 (Year 2)** – Copies of activity sheet 3, 'The Invasion of the Aliens!' and activity sheet, 'Message in Space' (Lesson resources CD-ROM).

Lesson/activity notes

- **Lesson** – Prepare the 'Plural pronoun cards' before the lesson. Use a large computer monitor to show 'Three blind mice' and display it for all the class to see.

- **Group 1 (Year 1)** – Children work as a discussion group with adult support writing out their sentences.

- **Group 2 (Year 1/2)** – Children work individually on activity sheet 2.1 and then in pairs on activity sheet 2.2.

- **Group 3 (Year 2)** – Children work in pairs or individually on activity sheet 3 depending on ability.

Lesson

Introduction

Display 'Three blind mice'. With the children read out the first original version. Now slowly read out the second version, pointing to the words at the same time. Ask the children what is different about this version. Some of the children may say 'Three blind mice' is used a lot', 'it doesn't rhyme' or 'there are too many words.' Underline the words 'Three blind mice' on the second version and ask the children what words have sometimes replaced them in the first version – they, their. Underline the words.

Main lesson

Explain to the children that the words 'they' and 'their' are called pronouns. Explain that a pronoun takes the place of a noun to make a sentence sound better. Highlight that the pronouns 'they' and 'their' replace plural nouns for

example, more than one person or object. Hold up the 'Plural pronoun cards' and, with the class, read out each word. Ask the children to think of a sentence using one of the plural pronouns. Write it on the board and read it out. Write a version without the pronoun. Discuss how the pronoun improves the sentence. Go through all the pronouns.

Explain to the children that they are going to investigate plural pronouns set in space. Put the children into their levelled groups. Spend time moving between the groups to discuss individual children's work and assess their level of understanding.

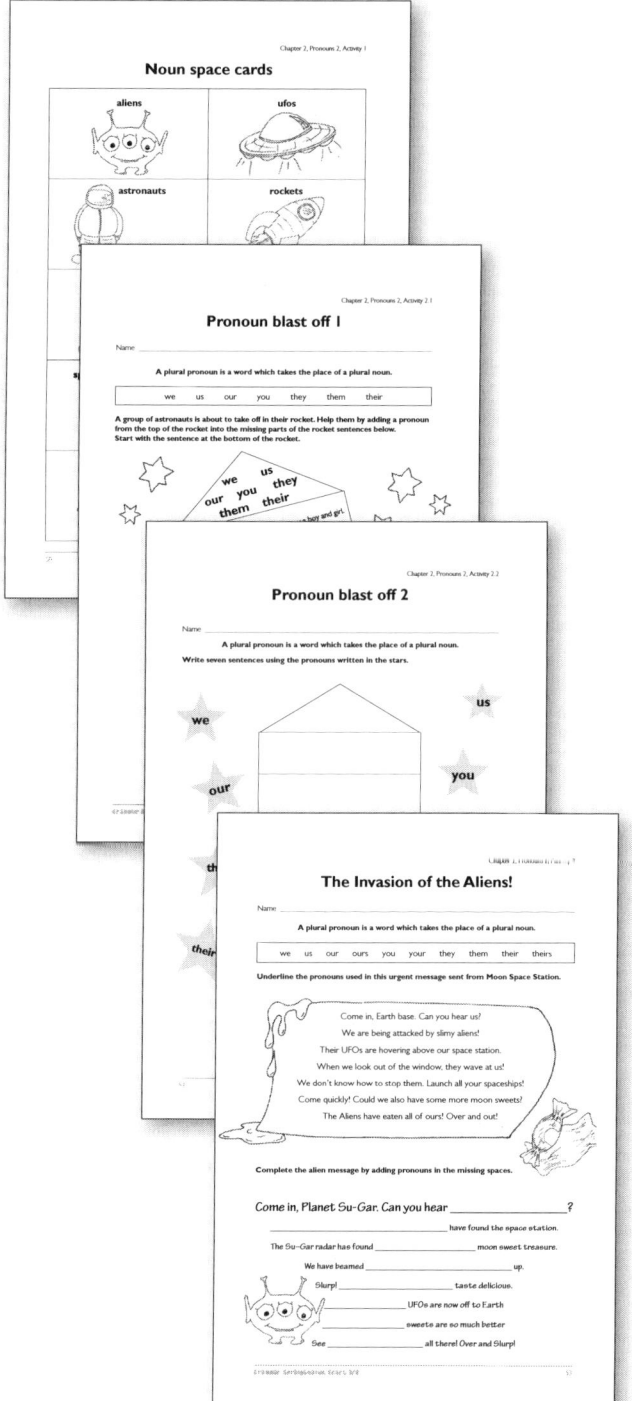

Activities

Group 1 (Year 1)

- Put one set of the 'Plural pronoun cards' face down in a pile in front of the children.

- Put one set of the 'Noun space cards' face down in a separate pile.

- Let the children take turns to turn over a pronoun card and a picture plural noun.

- Encourage them to create two sentences, the first using the picture noun and the second using the pronoun, e.g. *The UFOs were round. They looked pretty.*

- Write them out for the children to read or see. Do they make sense?

- Ask the children to circle the plural pronoun. Take note of their knowledge.

Group 2 (Year 1/2)

- Give out copies of activity sheet 'Pronoun blast off 1' to each child.

- Working individually, the children add missing pronouns to seven sentences.

- With the children, discuss how the pronouns improve the sentences.

- Give out the 'Pronoun blast off 2' sheet and ask the children to work in pairs to write seven simple sentences using the pronouns at the top of the rocket. The sentences don't have to be about space.

- Encourage the children to share their sentences with another pair or within the group.

Group 3 (Year 2)

- Give out copies of activity sheet 'Invasion of the Aliens!' to each child.

- Working individually, the children underline the pronouns in the astronaut message.

- They then add the correct pronouns to the alien message.

- Once they have completed the activity, ask the children to work in pairs to write a return message from either Earth Base or Planet Su-Gar using pronouns in their sentences. They can write it on, 'Message in space' activity sheet.

Plenary

At the end of the lesson, bring the groups together. Encourage the children to read out their pronoun sentences. Ask them what a pronoun word does. Show the plural pronoun cards again and remind the children that these are plural nouns and used to replace nouns that are more than one thing.

Support

For children who need extra support in identifying plural nouns, look at more nursery rhymes and simple poetry and discuss how they would sound without the plural pronouns.

Extension

Give the children a short fiction text and a short non-fiction text. Ask them to record the plural pronouns in each text and how many times each one is used. Discuss their findings. Ask where some pronouns are used more in a non-fiction text and vice versa.

Noun space cards

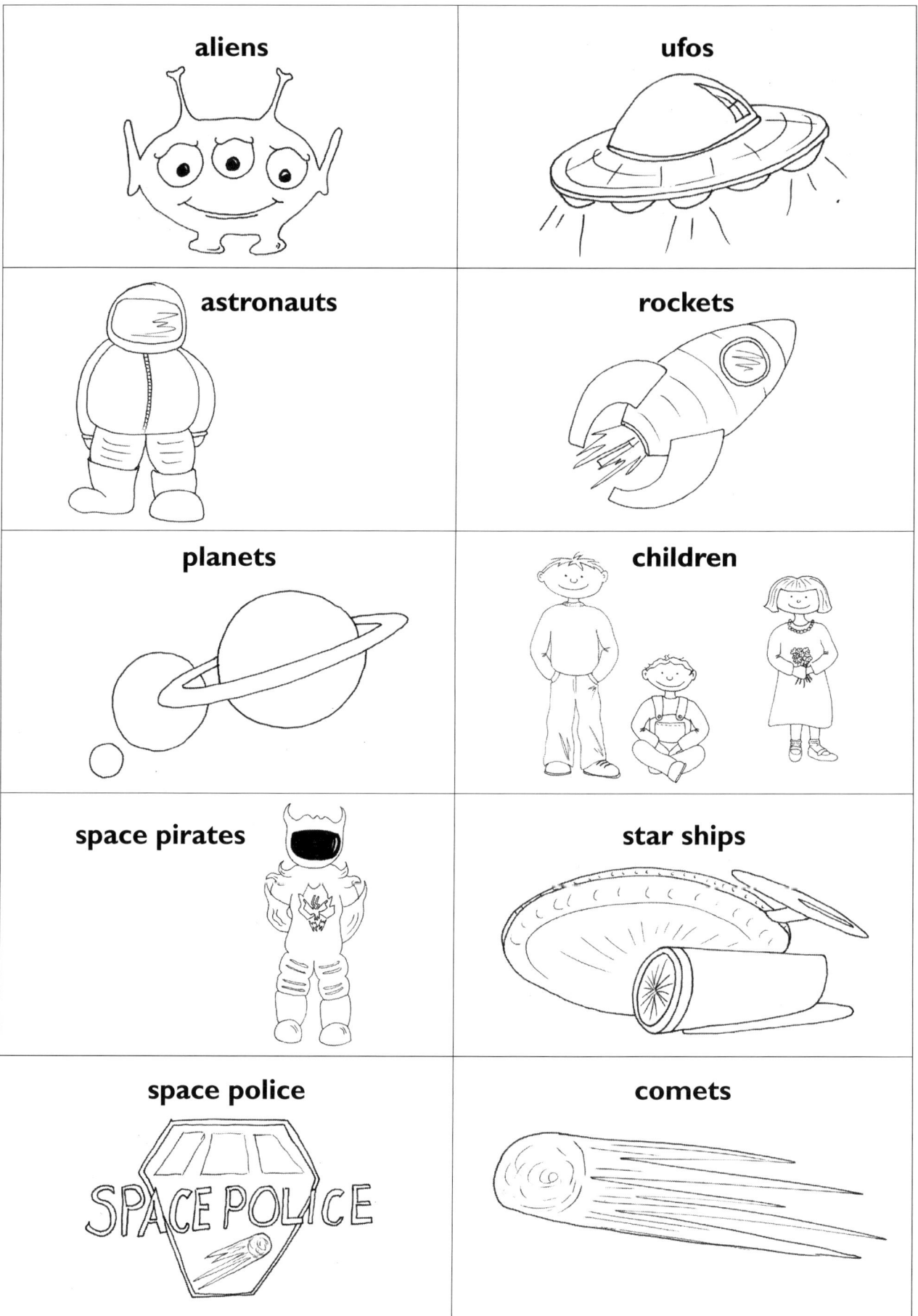

aliens	ufos
astronauts	rockets
planets	children
space pirates	star ships
space police	comets

Pronoun blast off 1

Name _____

A plural pronoun is a word which takes the place of a plural noun.

| we | us | our | you | they | them | their |

A group of astronauts is about to take off in their rocket. Help them by adding a pronoun from the top of the rocket into the missing parts of the rocket sentences below. Start with the sentence at the bottom of the rocket.

we   us
our   you   they
them   their

'I wish that was _____," say a boy and girl.

Blast off! People watch _____ zoom up into space.

"Yes, _____ are," say the astronauts.

"Are _____ all ready for take off?" ask Earth Control.

"We must put _____ seatbelts on," say the astronauts.

_____ shut the rocket door tightly.

The astronauts climb into _____ rocket.

Pronoun blast off 2

Name _____

A plural pronoun is a word which takes the place of a plural noun.

Write seven sentences using the pronouns written in the stars.

we

us

our

you

them

they

their

The Invasion of the Aliens!

Name _____

A plural pronoun is a word which takes the place of a plural noun.

| we | us | our | ours | you | your | they | them | their | theirs |

Underline the pronouns used in this urgent message sent from Moon Space Station.

Come in, Earth base. Can you hear us?

We are being attacked by slimy aliens!

Their UFOs are hovering above our space station.

When we look out of the window, they wave at us!

We don't know how to stop them. Launch all your spaceships!

Come quickly! Could we also have some more moon sweets?

The Aliens have eaten all of ours! Over and out!

Complete the alien message by adding pronouns in the missing spaces.

Come in, Planet Su-Gar. Can you hear _____?

_____ have found the space station.

The Su-Gar radar has found _____ moon sweet treasure.

We have beamed _____ up.

Slurp! _____ taste delicious.

_____ UFOs are now off to Earth

_____ sweets are so much better

See _____ all there! Over and Slurp!

Chapter 3 – Verbs

Verb Information

Verbs	Verbs are words that describe what nouns do or are. Verbs are very important. They form a main part of a sentence and give it a reason. Verbs bring ideas, events, places and people together. They enhance writing and can be used to great effect. Unlike other words, most verbs change in their form.		*lie, lay, laid.*
Main verbs These verbs describe what something or someone does or is.	**Action verbs**	play, kick, jump, drink, sleep.	*Katy played with her yo-yo.*
	Verbs describing a state	kind, seem, belong.	*The ball belonged to Joe.*
Helping verbs Can be used with main verbs. They have no meaning if used on their own. We usually use 'helping' verbs with main verbs. For example: *The children were eating a cake.* *I am riding my bike.*	**Being verbs** – these helping verbs show that a subject exists. are, am, is, was, were, been, being, be.	We use 'am' or 'was' if the subject of the sentence is 'I'.	*I am at my nan's.* *I was at my nan's.*
		We use 'is' or 'was', if the subject of the sentence is singular.	*Tim is sick.* *Tim was sick.*
		We use 'are' or 'were' if the subject of the sentence is plural.	*We are tired. We were tired.*
	Progressive form of verbs	The progressive form of a verb is used to describe events that are in progress. It is made by adding the 'being' verbs (am, is, are, was, were) in front of the verb's present participle '-ing' verbs. The choice of 'being' verb indicates the present or past tense of the sentence.	*I was eating a crunchy apple.* *I am eating a crunchy apple.* *We are eating crunchy apples.* *We were eating crunchy apples.*
		The progressive can also be used with the perfect.	*I have been eating a crunchy apple.*
	Having verbs	These helping verbs show what a subject has. has, have, having, had.	*Joe has a spot.* *Luke is having a bath.* *Molly had a bad tooth.*
	Saying verbs	Saying verbs describe how a subject talks or sounds.	*shout, roar, laugh, cry, whisper, call, say.*
	Singular and plural verbs Verbs can be singular or plural The basic rule is:	1.A singular verb is used with a singular subject	*The girl kicks a ball.*
		2.A plural verb is used with a plural subject.	*The girls kick a ball.*

Verb Information continued

Verb tenses Definition of tense – a way to tell the difference in time – past, present, future. Verbs change to show tenses when something happens or happened.	**Present tense**	What is happening now.	*Liam is drinking apple juice.*
	Regular present verb – present participle rule	1. Most verbs become present tense by adding '-ing' to the end of the word.	*sleep – sleeping* *kick – kicking*
		2. Regular verbs that end in '-e' must drop the '-e' before adding '-ing'.	*ride – riding* *bake – baking*
	Past tense	What has happened.	*I lost my purse when I went shopping.*
	Regular past verb – past participle rule	1. Most verbs become past tense by adding '-ed' to the end of the word.	*jump – jumped* *call – called*
		2. Regular verbs that end in '-e' must only add '-d' to the end of the word.	*dance – danced* *like – liked*
	Future tense	What is about to happen.	*Sara is going to see her friend next week.*
Regular and Irregular verbs	**Regular verbs**	Most verbs follow the simple past participle and present participle rules when changing tenses.	*look, looked, looking*
	Irregular verbs	The verbs change spelling in the past tense and past participle. There are no definite rules so they need to be learnt.	*buy, bought, go, went, see, saw*
	Imperative verbs	The imperative form of the verb gives a command. It is usually positioned at or near the beginning of the sentence.	*"Leave at once!" shouted the furious men.* *Write the date on the top line.*
	Changing verbs into nouns with the suffix '-er'	Nouns can sometimes be made when adding '-er' to verbs. If the verb ends with an '-e', drop the '-e' before adding '-er'.	*build – builder* *write – writer*
	Changing verb meanings using the prefix 'un-'	The prefix 'un-' can be added to the front of some verbs to show the opposite action.	*chain – unchain* *lock – unlock*

Verb objective chart

Objectives and year group	Action verbs	Past tense verbs ending in '-ed' or '-d'	Present tense verbs ending in '-ing'	Verbs starting with 'un-' prefix	Irregular verbs
Word – Year 1					
Recognise verbs.	★	★	★	★	★
Recognise adjectives.					
Suffixes that can be added to verbs – '-ing', '-ed', '-er'.		★	★		
How the prefix 'un-' changes the meaning of verbs (e.g. <u>un</u>tie the boat).				★	
Word – Year 2					
Use verbs.	★	★	★	★	★
Sentence – Year 1					
How words can combine to make sentences.			★	★	★
Joining words and joining clauses using 'and'.				★	
Sentence – Year 2					
Different sentences Statement, question, exclamation, command.	★	★	★	★	★
Text – Year 1					
Sequencing sentences to form short narrative.			★		★
Text – Year 2					
Use of present and past tense in writing.	★	★	★		★
Progressive form of verbs in present and past tense.	★		★		

Verb springboards

Word walls

Create eye catching word walls. One flash card equals one brick. Have several bricks to create the word wall with the children. The walls can be used in a variety of ways. Have blank cards that the children can write new verbs and add to or make a new word wall shape. Use them as games with the children for example, sorting the words into the right pairs.

- Action verbs – action verbs in categories such as sports, hobbies.

- Saying verbs – different saying verbs that could replace 'said'.

- Past tense verbs – pairs of base verbs with '-ed' ending words or base words with '-d' ending verbs.

- Present tense verbs – pairs of base verbs with '-ing' verbs.

- Irregular pairs of verbs.

The word ladder

A similar game to 'Consequences'. In groups of four the children are given strips of paper with four sections (see Word ladder Template – Teacher resources on CD-ROM). The children write a verb on the first section, fold over the paper to hide it and pass it to the next child. They then write another verb on the next and so on. After the strip has been completed it is opened up and the children read out the four written verbs.

- The game can be used for action verbs where the children create a short story sequence or recount using the verbs or making simple sentences. Saying verbs – the children use the saying verbs to create speaking characters.

Word wheel/ word slide

(see Teacher resources on CD-ROM for templates)
The teacher or children add verbs to the wheels or slides to explore how verbs change when they become simple past and present tense verbs. Also a good reinforcement resource.

Missing verbs

Make copies of a fictional or non–fictional text and blank out the verbs (could be all or specific such as saying verbs, past tense '-ed' verbs). Give copies to a group of children and ask them to list the verbs that they think are missing. Compare the verb lists with the other groups.

Story telling circle

Each child is given or told a saying verb. A story is started with a dialogue sentence. The next children in the circle add their own dialogue sentence to the story in the verbal expression of their saying verb.

Other activity ideas

- Listen and look at the lyrics of action rhymes, such as 'Here we go round the Mulberry Bush', 'London's Burning', and 'Farmer's in his den'.

- Play action game such as 'Simon says...' or 'O'Grady says...' Adapt it to saying verbs and the children have to say a set sentence in the style of the saying verb.

- Alphabet verb lists.

- Children writing explanatory texts of a topic highlighting present tense '-ing' verbs.

- The children draw pin people or verb badges to go with action verbs.

- Creating or solving word searches, solving puzzles.

- Ten minute challenge to make a list of as many verbs as possible. Categories include action verbs, saying verbs, past or present tense verbs or irregular pairs of verbs.

- Take photos of the children doing something. Print them and turn them into a verb book with sentence captions under each picture. Highlight the verbs.

- Create displays of verb categories with labels and captions. For example draw large outlines of a boy and girl and show the verbs related to the body – *sniff*, *run*, and *sneeze*. Have pockets of labels to show the past and present tense version of each verb.

- Create antonym and synonym verbs displays. Use mobiles or 3D models to encourage the children to look at the words.

- Speech bubble fun. Use the speech bubble templates or make your own. Ask the children in groups or pairs to write a dialogue sentence spoken in the style of a given saying verb.

Action verbs

Learning objectives

- To understand that a verb shows what something or someone does.

- To understand that some verbs describe actions.

- To identify and use action verbs.

Resources

- **Lesson** – 'The word web' template if needed. (Teacher resources CD-ROM)

- **Group 1 (Year 1)** – Copies of activity sheet 1 'Sports' for each child.

- **Group 2 (Year 1/2)** – Copies of activity sheet 2 'Hobbies' for each child. Copies of 'The word web' for each pair of children.

- **Group 3 (Year 2)** – Copies of activity sheet 3 'Using 'to be' verbs' for each child.

Lesson/activity notes

- **Lesson** – Make sure the children are away from the furniture when playing 'Simon says'.

- **Group 1 (Year 1)** – Children work as a discussion group with adult support.

- **Group 2 (Year 1/2)** – Children work individually and then in pairs. The group may need adult support

- **Group 3 (Year 2)** – Children work individually and then pair–share word searches.

Lesson

Introduction

Play the game 'Simon says' with all the class. Choose action verbs such as, 'Simon says...run, jump, skip, hop, march etc.' Finish the game with the action verb 'sit'. Once all the children have sat down, explain that all the action words are called verbs. Say that verbs are words that show what something or someone does. Write the verbs used in the game. Explain that these verbs are called action verbs as they show different actions.

Main lesson

Draw a verb web on the board (see 'The Word Web' template) and write the title 'Action verbs' in the middle. Add an action verb. Ask each child for an example of an action verb and add it to the web, *walk, jump, crawl, ski*. Once the action verb web is full, explain that they are going to make an action verb list poem. Start by writing a

simple line with your verb: *Charlie likes to crawl on his knees.* Highlight the alliteration and the verb. Let the children say their action verb sentences and write them on the board as a list, *Joe likes to jump in the air.* Read out the action verb list poem with the children.

Explain to the children that they are going to do action verb activities. Put the children into their levelled groups and give out the activities. Spend time moving between the groups to discuss individual children's work and assess their level of understanding.

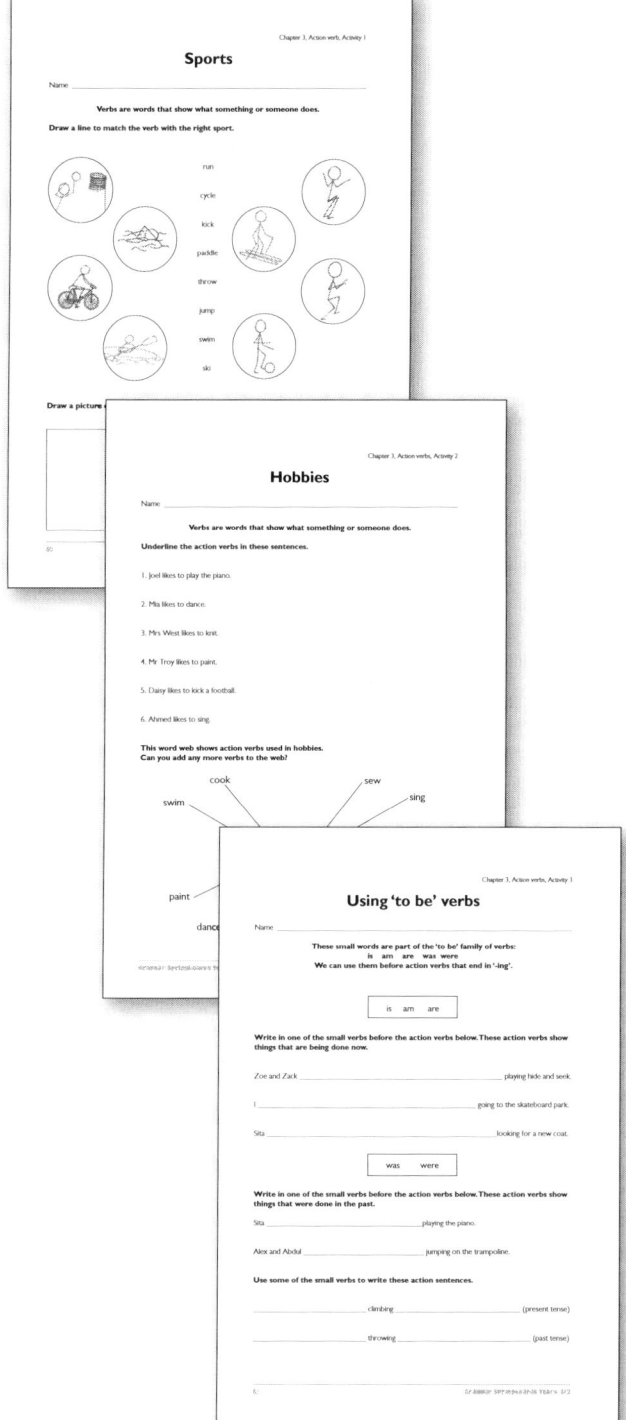

Activities

Group 1 (Year 1)

- Give out copies of the activity sheet 'Sports' to each of the children.

- As a discussion group, go through the pictures with the children and ask what sport they represent. Highlight how each picture shows an action.

- Read through the action verbs at the side and ask the children to link the right action verb to the right sport.
- Encourage each of the children to draw a picture of a sport and help them if needed to write the action verb underneath the picture.

Group 2 (Year 1/2)

- Give out copies of the activity sheet 'Hobbies' to each child.

- Discuss with the children their favourite hobbies. Highlight action verbs used in the hobbies, *play, knit, kick*.

- Working individually, the children underline the action verbs in sentences about hobbies.

- They then add a few more action verbs to a word web on hobbies and use the web to add the missing action verbs into three sentences.

- If time, put the children in pairs and give them a blank copy of 'The word web'. Ask them to list action verbs for their favourite hobby. How many verbs can they list?

Group 3 (Year 2)

- Give each child a copy of activity sheet 3, 'Using 'to be' verbs'. Read out the text at the top of the sheet and read out the 'to be' verbs. Ask children to point to the '-ing' action verbs before the gaps where the 'to be' verbs need to be added. Discuss how the sentences show an action actually taking place.

- Working individually, children add the correct 'to be' verbs for present and past tense sentences.

- They then write a present tense sentence and a past tense sentence using 'to be' verbs.

Plenary

Before the end of the lesson bring all the groups back together. Ask the children for examples of action verbs they have been working on. Ask the children what an action verb is – an action or doing word. If time, play a game of action verb charades. Choose one or two children to mime an action verb for the class to guess.

Support

To give children more support on action verbs, help them create a simple comic strip recount of a journey, a game, or an activity that they have experienced. With the children write simple sentences underneath each picture frame with an action verb.

Extension

Encourage the children to read a short adventure story and record the action verbs used in the text. Discuss how the action verbs make the story exciting. Suggest they create and act out an adventure sequence using different actions and get others to guess the verbs.

Sports

Name _____

Verbs are words that show what something or someone does.

Draw a line to match the verb with the right sport.

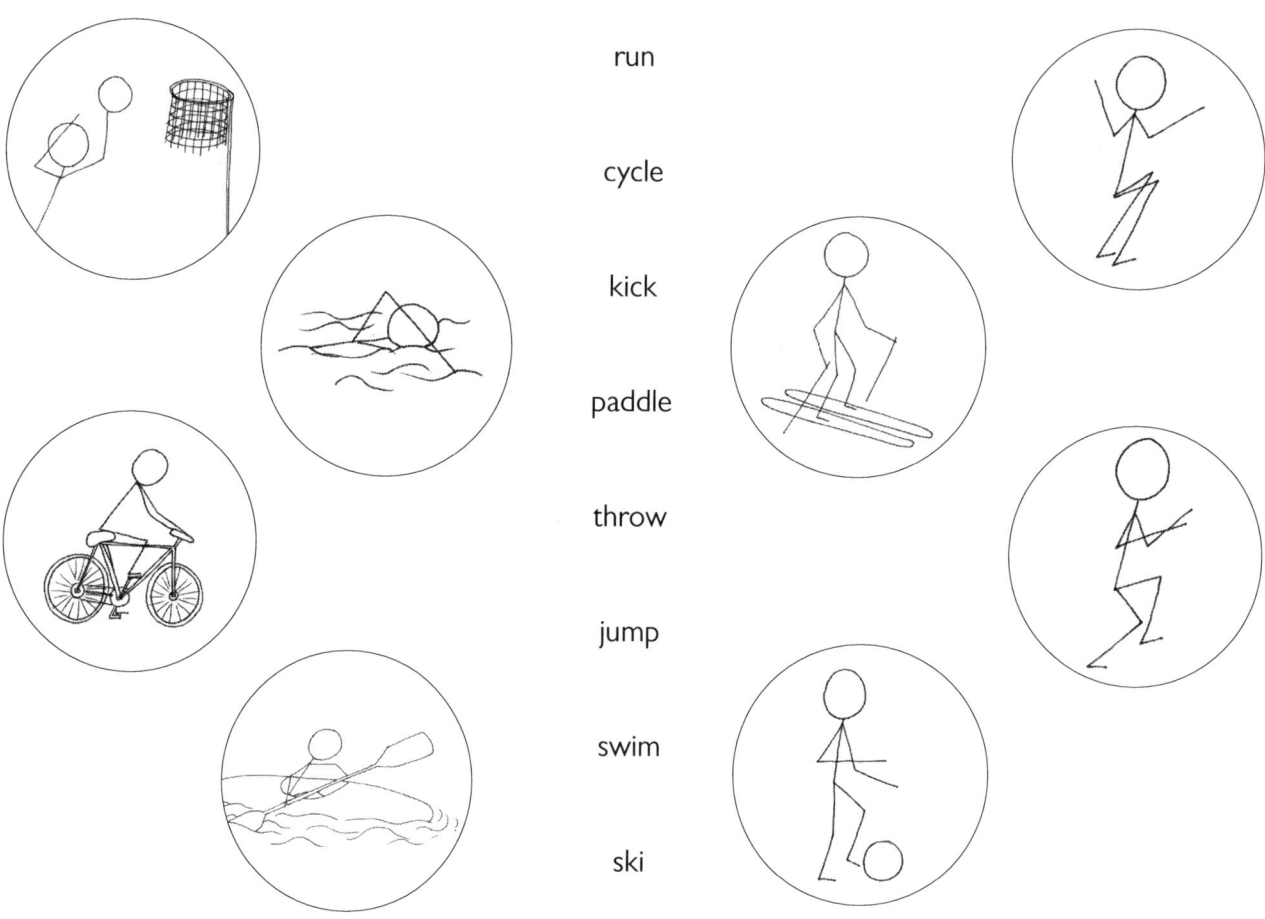

run

cycle

kick

paddle

throw

jump

swim

ski

Draw a picture of an action verb in the box below. Write the verb on the line.

Hobbies

Name _____

Verbs are words that show what something or someone does.

Underline the action verbs in these sentences.

1. Joel likes to play the piano.

2. Mia likes to dance.

3. Mrs West likes to knit.

4. Mr Troy likes to paint.

5. Daisy likes to kick a football.

6. Ahmed likes to sing.

This word web shows action verbs used in hobbies.
Can you add any more verbs to the web?

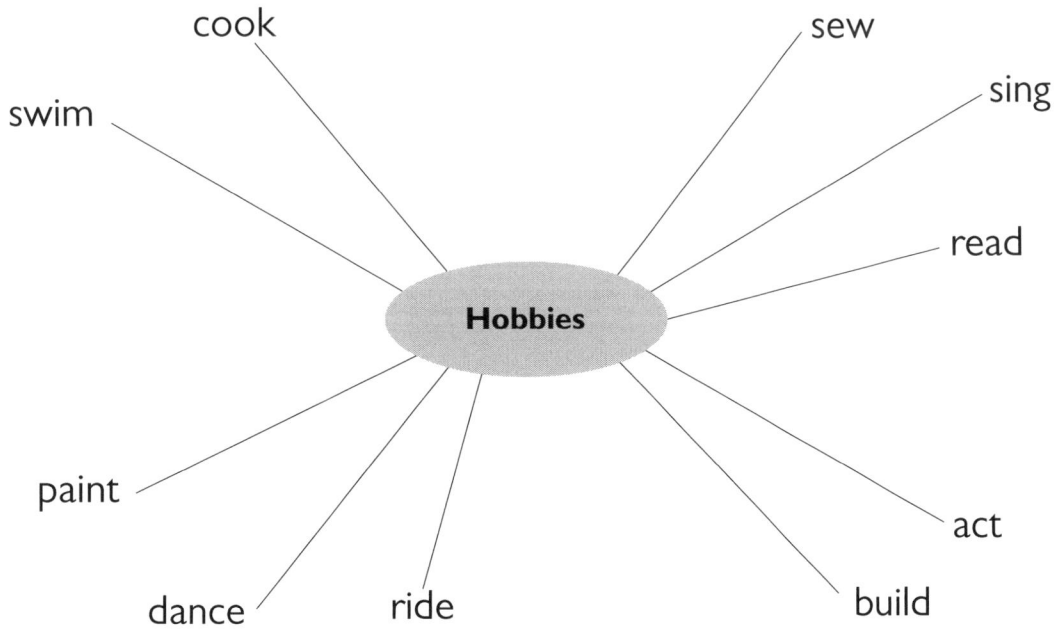

Using 'to be' verbs

Name _____

These small words are part of the 'to be' family of verbs:
is   am   are   was   were
We can use them before action verbs that end in '-ing'.

is	am	are

Write in one of the small verbs before the action verbs below. These action verbs show things that are being done now.

Zoe and Zack _____ playing hide and seek.

I _____ going to the skateboard park.

Sita _____ looking for a new coat.

was	were

Write in one of the small verbs before the action verbs below. These action verbs show things that were done in the past.

Sita _____ playing the piano.

Alex and Abdul _____ jumping on the trampoline.

Use some of the small verbs to write these action sentences.

_____ climbing _____ (present tense)

_____ throwing _____ (past tense)

Past tense verbs ending in '-ed' or '-d'

Learning objectives
- To understand that verbs can describe actions that happened in the past.

- To change simple verb into past tense by adding '-ed' or '-d' if the verb ends in '-e'.

- To recognise and use simple past tense verbs ending in '-ed' and '-d'.

Resources
- **Lesson** – 'Verb cards 1', 'Verb cards 2', '-ed' and '-d' cards, 'Nothing much' – (Lesson resources CD-ROM)

- **Group 1 (Year 1)** – One copy of activity sheet 1, 'Past tense verb card activity' to be turned into cards. Two tins or small boxes with '-ed' on one and '-d' on the other.

- **Group 2 (Year 1/2)** – Copies of activity sheet 2, 'Past tense verbs ending in '-ed' and '-d'' for each child.

- **Group 3 (Year 2)** – Copies of activity sheet 3 'Past tense verbs' for each child.

Lesson/activity notes
- **Group 1 (Year 1)** – Children work as a discussion group with an adult.

- **Group 2 (Year 1/2)** – Children work individually and then in pairs.

- **Group 3 (Year 2)** – Children work individually.

Lesson

Introduction
Draw a table with the headings of the seven days of the week written down the side. Display the 'Verb cards 1 and 2' for the children to see. Highlight that they are verbs. Explain that most verbs can show actions in the past by adding '-ed' onto their end. Put the '-ed' card next to 'Verb cards 1' and read out each past tense verb. Point to 'Verb cards 2' and highlight that these verbs all end with '-e' so the children only need to add '-d' onto the end. Put the '-d' card next to the verbs and with the children read out each past tense verb.

Main lesson
Read the story 'Nothing much' to the children. Write a few of the past tense verbs on the board, such as chased, climbed. Underline the '-ed' and '-d' on the verbs. Say that

as a class the children are going to create a fun recount of a week by turning the verb cards into past actions. Starting on Monday, show the first verb card and ask if it should have an '-ed' or '-d' on the end. Ask the children for an activity and write their ideas as sentences. Once the activity is completed, read through the story with the children and underline the past tense verbs.

Explain to the children that they are going to do activities using verbs showing past actions. Put the children into their levelled groups and give out the activities. Spend time moving between the groups to discuss individual children's work and assess their level of understanding.

Activities

Group 1 (Year 1)

- Put out the two tins or boxes and the shuffled verb cards face down on the table.

- Working as a group, the children take turns to pick up a verb card and read it out.

- Ask the children what the verb is as a past action, for example 'rain' becomes 'rained'.

- Ask what they need to add onto the end of the verb to make it a past action '-ed' or '-d' and then put it in the correct tin.

- Once all the cards are in the tins, empty them out and go through each verb reinforcing the endings.

- In pairs ask the children to create an oral recount of a special day such as day trip or a birthday using some of the verbs.

Group 2 (Year 1/2)

- Give out copies of the activity sheet 2 'Past tense verbs ending in '-ed' and '-d'' to the children.

- Working individually, the children change two lists of verbs into past tense by adding '-ed' or '-d'.

- They then complete four sentences that show four activities at a fair by adding missing verbs from a choice listed on the sheet.

- Once the children have completed the sheet, they can draw in the activities.

Group 3 (Year 2)

- Give out copies of the activity sheet 3, 'Past tense verbs,' to each of the children.

- Working individually, the children complete a fictional recount by writing the correct past tense verbs from a given word box.

- The children then, on a separate piece of paper, write what happened next in the story. Allow them to say their sentences before they write them down.

- Ask them to underline all the past tense verbs in their story. Have they used '-ed' and '-d' correctly?

- Encourage the children to retell their recounts to the other pairs in their group and ask them to make notes of past tense verbs.

Plenary

At the end of the lesson, bring the groups together and discuss their various activities. Write the verb 'jump' on the board and ask the children what they need to add to the word to make it a past action or past tense. They should say '-ed'.

Write the verb, 'move' on the board and ask the children what they need to add to the word to make it a past action or past tense. They should say 'just '-d' as '-e' is already there'.

Support

Use a simple reading text or recount such as a traditional tale and help the children find verbs that end in '-ed' and '-d'. Write them out on a white board and ask the children to underline the '-ed' or '-d' of each verb.

Extension

Encourage the children to write their own recounts of something they have done in the past. Encourage them to make a word bank of the past tense '-ed' verbs that they come across or use. Highlight that some past tense verbs do not follow simple rules, such as see, saw.

Past tense verb card activity

jump	dance
look	smile
cook	move
play	wipe
pull	chase
shout	sneeze
walk	tickle

Past tense verbs ending in '-ed' or '-d'

Name _____

Most verbs can describe past actions by adding '-ed' or '-d'
lick – licked, wiggle – wiggled.

Turn these verbs into past actions by adding '-ed' or '-d'.

play played	smile smiled

A day at the funfair

Complete the sentences by adding the correct past tense verbs from the box below. Draw the pictures for each sentence.

Pip and Thea _____ large ice creams.	Tom and Layla _____ on the trampoline.
Abdul and Joe _____in a row boat.	Mel and Zak _____the juggler.

licked	paddled	jumped	watched

Past tense verbs

Name _____

Most verbs can describe past actions by adding '-ed' or '-d'
lick – licked, wiggle – wiggled.

The snowman surprise

Add the correct past tense verbs from the box below to complete the story.

The clock _____ seven o'clock. I _____

out of bed and _____ out of the window. It had _____.

I got _____ and _____

the door. I _____ the snow until it was a big snowman.

As I _____ back to the house, a snowball _____

me on the head. My snowman had _____ and in his hand he had a snowball.

jumped	chimed	dressed	bumped	walked	snowed
	smiled	opened	moved	pushed	

What happened next? Write the rest of the story. Underline any '-ed' or '-d' verbs you may have used.

_____

_____

_____

_____

Present tense verbs ending with '-ing'

Learning objectives

- To change a regular verb into present tense by adding '-ing'.

- To understand that when '-ing' is added to verbs ending in '-e', the '-e' is dropped.

- To recognise and use simple present tense verbs ending with '-ing'.

Resources

- **Lesson** – "-ing' verb machine template' "-ing' verb slide list' "-ing' slide strips' – (Lesson resources CD-ROM)

- **Group 1 (Year 1)** – A variety of photos/pictures of action verbs for simple '-ing' rules, *pull*, *jump*, *walk*. Colouring pens, paper for labels.

- **Group 2 (Year 1/2)** – Copies of activity sheet 1 'Match the '-ing' verbs' for each child.

- **Group 3 (Year 2)** – Copies of activity sheet 2 'Present tense verbs' for each child.

Lesson/activity notes

- **Lesson** – Before the lesson cut out and create the "-ing' verb machine'. Copy or make the two card strips. Have a copy of the "-ing' verb slide lists' near you.

- **Group 1 (Year 1)** – Children work as a discussion group with an adult. Record their responses and choices during the activity.

- **Group 2 (Year 1/2)** – Children work individually and then in pairs.

- **Group 3 (Year 2)** – Children work individually.

the rest of the class to guess. When the class have guessed the action write the verb on the appropriate strip of card for all the children to see (Strip 1=verbs ending without an '-e', Strip 2=verbs with an '-e' ending.) Show the '-ing' verb machine' and point to the '-ing'. Thread in Strip 1 and pull the strip and with the children say out the words. Show Strip 2 and highlight that all these verbs end with '-e'. Explain that when adding '-ing' to a verb which ends in '-e', they must drop the '-e'. Use a pen to cross out the '-e's and pull the strip through the '-ing' machine. Read out the verbs.

Explain to the children that they are going to do activities with '-ing' verbs. Put the children into their levelled groups and give out the activities. Spend time moving between the groups to discuss individual children's work and assess their level of understanding.

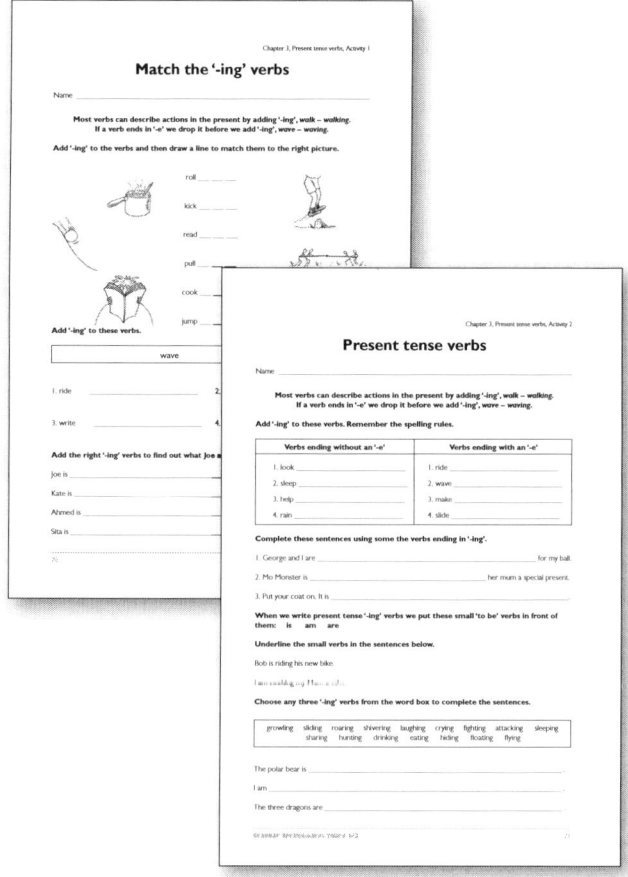

Lesson

Introduction

Put the children into groups of two or three. Explain that they are going to play a game using verbs. Highlight how verbs can tell us when things are happening in the past, the future and the present. Explain that the present is what is happening now. Ask *'What is happening now?'* The children could answer, *'We are listening,'* *'You are talking.'* Highlight how the children were adding '-ing' to the end of the present tense verbs.

Main lesson

Give each group a verb from the "-ing' verb slide lists'. Explain that each group must act out the verb action for

Activities

Group 1 (Year 1)

- With the children cut out pictures/photos from magazines to show different verb actions.

- On paper, create labels of the base verb under the relevant pictures/photos, such as jump, walk, smile.

- With the children sort out the labels into piles of verbs that end in '-e' and verbs that don't end in '-e'.

- Look at verbs which don't end in '-e' and write '-ing' on the end of one.

- Encourage the children to take turns to write '-ing' on the rest of the verbs.

- Look at the pile of verbs ending in '-e'. Show by example the rule of cutting '-e' and adding '-ing'. Ask the children to add '-ing' to the rest of these verbs.

- Ask the children to choose one of the verbs from each pile and draw their own pictures of the verbs. Encourage them to write their own labels.

Group 2 (Year 1/2)
- Give the children copies of the activity sheet 1 'Match the '-ing' verbs.'

- Working individually, the children add '-ing' to verbs that do not end in '-e' and then match the verbs to the right pictures showing the verb actions.

- They then add '-ing' to four verbs ending in '-e'.

- They complete the activity sheet by using some of the verbs to complete four sentences.

- At the end of the activity, go over the verbs to reinforce the children's learning.

Group 3 (Year 2)
- Give a copy of activity sheet 3 'Present tense verbs' to each child.

- Working individually, the children must add '-ing' to verbs that end with '-e' and verbs that do not end with '-e'.

- They then use some of the '-ing' verbs to complete four sentences.

- The children then underline the 'to be' verbs in sentences and write three sentences using three '-ing' verbs from a word box.

- If time, let the children create their own '-ing' verb wheels using a blank wheel template and ask a partner to make sentences.

Plenary
Before the end of the lesson, bring the groups together and ask them to give examples of verbs that end in '-ing'. Ask the children what they must do to verbs which end in '-e' before they add '-ing' Write their examples on the board.

Support
For those children that need more support, create a word bank of verbs that end in '-ing' and those that have an '-e' taken off before an '-ing'. Encourage the children to draw pictures to go with each verb.

Extension
Encourage the children to find more '-ing' verbs and encourage them to create poster word lists which they can add to as they identify and discover more regular present verbs.

Match the '-ing' verbs

Name _____

Most verbs can describe actions in the present by adding '-ing', *walk – walking.*
If a verb ends in '-e' we drop it before we add '-ing', *wave – waving.*

Add '-ing' to the verbs and then draw a line to match them to the right picture.

roll ___ ___ ___

kick ___ ___ ___

read ___ ___ ___

pull ___ ___ ___

cook ___ ___ ___

jump ___ ___ ___

Add '-ing' to these verbs.

wave	waving

1. ride _____   2. chase _____

3. write _____   4. dance _____

Add the right '-ing' verbs to find out what Joe and his friends are doing.

Joe is _____ a cake.

Kate is _____ a book.

Ahmed is _____ a bike.

Sita is _____ a letter.

Present tense verbs

Name _____

**Most verbs can describe actions in the present by adding '-ing', *walk – walking*.
If a verb ends in '-e' we drop it before we add '-ing', *wave – waving*.**

Add '-ing' to these verbs. Remember the spelling rules.

Verbs ending without an '-e'	Verbs ending with an '-e'
1. look _____	1. ride _____
2. sleep _____	2. wave _____
3. help _____	3. make _____
4. rain _____	4. slide _____

Complete these sentences using some the verbs ending in '-ing'.

1. George and I are _____ for my ball.

2. Mo Monster is _____ her mum a special present.

3. Put your coat on. It is _____.

When we write present tense '-ing' verbs we put these small 'to be' verbs in front of them: is   am   are

Underline the small verbs in the sentences below.

Bob is riding his new bike.

I am cooking my Mum a cake.

Choose any three '-ing' verbs from the word box to complete the sentences.

growling   sliding   roaring   shivering   laughing   crying   fighting   attacking   sleeping
sharing   hunting   drinking   eating   hiding   floating   flying

The polar bear is _____ .

I am _____ .

The three dragons are _____ .

Verbs starting with 'un-' prefix

Learning objectives
- To understand what a prefix means.

- To understand how the prefix 'un-' can change the meaning of verbs.

- To discover verbs that can have 'un-' put in front of them.

Resources
- **Lesson** – Cut out verbs and 'un-' verbs from activity sheets 1.1. and 1.2. A display of the verbs for all the children to use as reference.

- **Group 1 (Year 1)** – Cut up cards from the activity sheets 1.1 'Matching 'un-' verb opposites' and 1.2 'Matching 'un-' verb opposites' for each child or a couple of sets for a small group or pair.

- **Group 2 (Year 1/2)** – Cut up cards from the activity sheets 1.1 and 1.2 'Matching 'un-' verb opposites' for each child or a couple of sets for a small group or pair. Paper and writing implements.

- **Group 3 (Year 2)** – Copies of activity sheet 2, 'Making opposite verbs from the prefix 'un-' for each child. Colouring pencils.

Lesson/activity notes
- **Lesson** – The children work individually, or in pairs or threes, to carry out the miming activity.

- **Group 1 (Year 1)** – Children work as a group or in pairs with adult support.

- **Group 2 (Year 1/2)** – Children work in pairs or individually.

- **Group 3 (Year 2)** – Children work individually.

Lesson

Introduction
Remind the children what a verb is. Explain how some verbs can change their meaning by adding a set of short words in front of them. Explain that these short words are called prefixes. Introduce the prefix 'un-' and say the sound. Let the children say the sound of the prefix after you.

Main lesson
Write the verb 'to button' on the board. Ask children for examples of when we use the verb, for example: to button up a coat, to button up a cardigan. Explain that you are

going to add the prefix 'un-' in front of button to change its meaning. Once you have done it, ask the children what it means. Highlight how the 'un-' undoes the action of the original verb.

Give out a verb or 'un-' verb card to each child or children in twos or threes. Ask them to think of how to mime the action of their verb. Display all the verbs on the board so the children can choose what the verb being mimed may be.

Explain to the children that they are now going to work on activities to do with the prefix 'un-'.

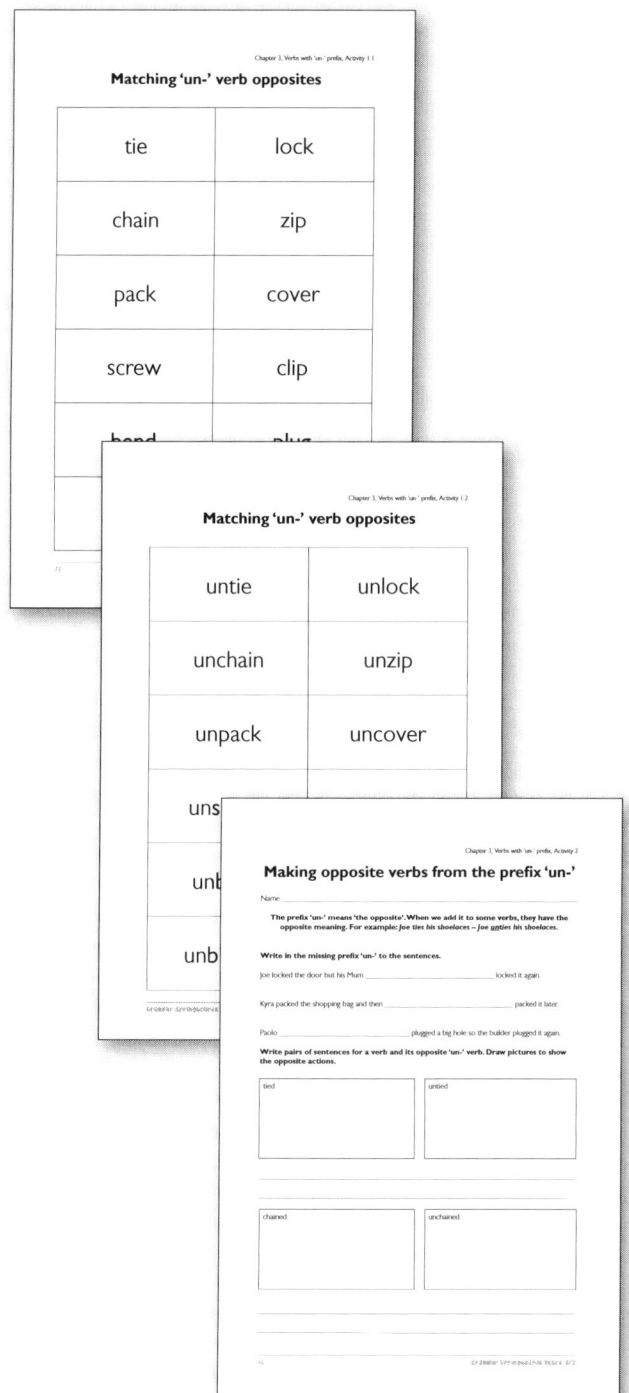

Activities

Group 1 (Year 1)

• Have the children in a small group or in pairs.

• Use the cards to play various games such as matching pairs where the children put the pair cards together or they lay out the verb cards and use a pile of prefix 'un-' cards to place on top.

• Let the children choose one pair of verbs (with prefix and without) and orally describe examples of the verb being used, such as a door being locked or unlocked.

Group 2 (Year 1/2)

• Put the children in pairs and give them a pile of verb cards and a pile of prefix verb cards.

• Ask the pairs to play a matching snap style game.

• Then choose a pair of verbs and ask them to say sentences using them followed by writing the sentences out.

• Encourage the pair to share their sentences with other pairs. Ask 'Can you think of other verbs that can have a prefix in front of them?' Let the children list their words.

Group 3 (Year 2)

• Give out the copies of 'Making opposite verbs from the prefix 'un-' for each child.

• Make sure the children read the information and look at the example at the top of the sheet.

• Working individually, the children add the prefix to change verbs in three sentences. Before they move to the next exercise, let the children discuss how the prefix affects the meaning of the sentences – undoing of a verb.

• They then write four simple sentences using two verbs and their 'un-' prefix equivalent. Pictures can be drawn to show the verb actions.

Plenary

Ten minutes before the end of the lesson, bring all the children together. Let them share their work with each other. Remind the children what a prefix is and how 'un-' can undo the actions of certain verbs. Highlight that this does not happen to all verbs.

Support

Continue with using games such as pairs, matching and bingo style activities to help children identify verbs with 'un-'.

Extension

Encourage the children to create a word bank of verbs that can have the 'un-' prefix in front of it.

Matching 'un-' verb opposites

tie	lock
chain	zip
pack	cover
screw	clip
bend	plug
button	wind

Matching 'un-' verb opposites

untie	unlock
unchain	unzip
unpack	uncover
unscrew	unclip
unbend	unplug
unbutton	unwind

Making opposite verbs from the prefix 'un-'

Name _____

The prefix 'un-' means 'the opposite'. When we add it to some verbs, they have the opposite meaning. For example: *Joe ties his shoelaces – Joe <u>un</u>ties his shoelaces.*

Write in the missing prefix 'un-' to the sentences.

Joe locked the door but his Mum _____ locked it again.

Kyra packed the shopping bag and then _____ packed it later.

Paolo _____ plugged a big hole so the builder plugged it again.

Write pairs of sentences for a verb and its opposite 'un-' verb. Draw pictures to show the opposite actions.

tied	untied

_____

_____

chained	unchained

_____

_____

Irregular verbs

Learning objectives
- To understand that some verbs don't follow simple rules of adding '-ed' or '-d' to become past tense.

- To understand that verbs that have different spellings when describing past actions are called irregular verbs.

- To recognise and use simple common irregular verbs and their past tense.

Resources
- **Lesson** – A display area or board, 'Word wall base verbs' and 'Word wall past tense irregular verbs.' (Lesson resources CD-ROM). Sticking product such as velcro, pins to hold word wall cards to display area.

- **Group 1 (Year 1)** – Activity sheets 1 and 2 'Irregular verbs pairs'. Board or table to display a word wall.

- **Group 2 (Year 1/2)** – Activity sheets 1 and 2 'Irregular verbs pairs'. Small or large whiteboard and pen.

- **Group 3 (Year 2)** – Activity sheet 3, 'Irregular verbs wall'. word bank, word wall design ideas. (Teacher resources CD-ROM)

Lesson/activity notes
- **Lesson** – Choose an area to create a word wall to display the pairs of irregular verbs. Create the word wall base verbs and past tense irregular verb cards and make sure they are mixed up and on display for all the children to see. Leave a slight gap between the pair cards on the word wall so the children don't confuse the different pairs of verbs. The wall should be three pairs along and four pairs high.

- **Group 1 (Year 1)** – Children work as a discussion group with adult support. Colour code the pairs of cards for children who have reading difficulties.

- **Group 2 (Year 1/2)** – Children work as a discussion group with adult support and then two small groups.

- **Group 3 (Year 2)** – Children work individually on the activity sheet and then in twos or threes.

Lesson

Introduction
Remind the children that verbs show what something or someone does. Remind the children how some verbs can have '-ed' to show past actions. Highlight to the children that not all verbs follow these simple rules. Some verbs change their letters in the middle, some don't change at all and some have a totally different word. Write on the board – 'I see the sky.' The verb 'see' doesn't become 'seed' for a past action. We use the word 'saw'. 'I saw the sky.'

Main lesson
Explain to the children that these types of verbs are called irregular verbs. Tell children that they are going to help you make a word wall using pairs of irregular verbs. Hold up the first base verb card and ask the children to read it out, for example, see. Ask the children how they would say that verb for a past event. *We saw a fish.* Ask the children to see if they can find the verb card 'saw' on the display. If the children need support, read out the verbs and ask them to stop you when you say 'saw'. Put the 'see' and 'saw' cards at the bottom of the wall. Carry on with the activity until you have the word wall.

Explain to the children that they are going to do more activities with irregular verbs. Put the children into their levelled groups and give out the activities. Spend time moving between the groups to discuss individual children's work and assess their level of understanding.

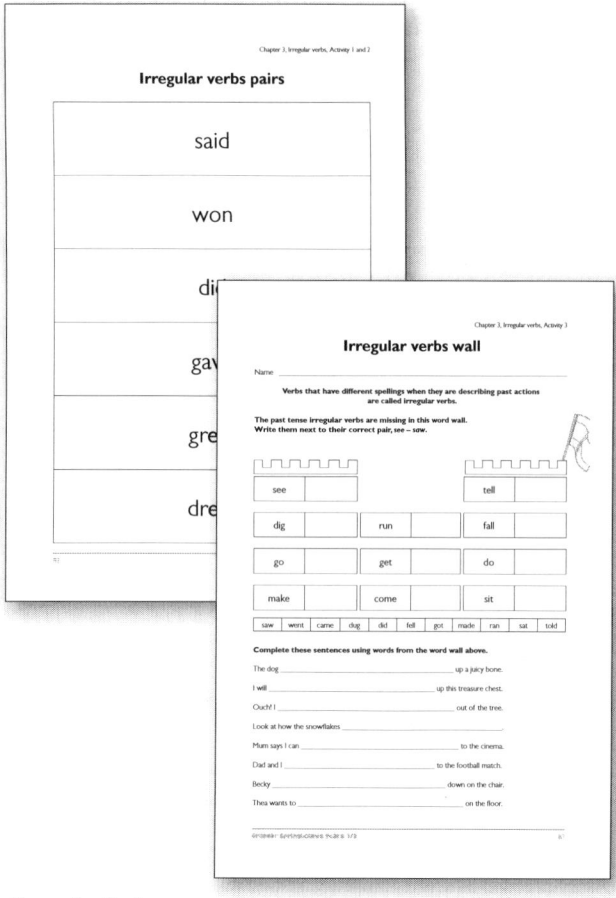

Activities

Group 1 (Year 1)

- Show the children one pair of base and past tense verb cards such as see/saw and say two sentences using them.

- Spread out the past tense verb cards on a table or floor.

- Give each child one or two of the base verb cards and ask them to find either its matching colour card or a verb that would describe the same action in the past.

- When the pairs have been found, explain that they are going to make a castle word wall using their pairs of irregular verbs.

- Ask each child in turn to display their pairs and with the group, make simple sentences using them.

- Once the castle word wall is made, use it to help reinforce the words. *Can you find me the verb, 'sat'? How is it different from 'sit'?*

Group 2 (Year 1/2)

- Show the children one pair of base and past tense verb cards such as see/saw and say two sentences using them.

- Mix up the cards and ask the children in turn to find a verb and its past tense pair.

- Go round the children in turn until all the pairs are found.

- Look at each pair with the children and make sentences using them by writing them on a small or large white board.

- Reinforce verb recognition by playing a game of 'Pairs'. Shuffle all the cards and lay out them face down. The children take turns to turn over two cards to find the pair of verbs. They turn them back if not the right pair.

Group 3 (Year 2)

- Remind the children how some verbs have different spellings when they describe past actions, for instance see/saw. Use the lesson word wall as reference.

- Give each of the children a copy of the activity sheet 'Irregular verbs wall'.

- The children must add the correct past tense verbs from a box to complete the pairs on a word wall.

- They then use some of the verbs from the word wall to complete six sentences.

- If time, encourage the children to work in twos or threes to think of some more examples of simple irregular verbs (see word bank) and create word wall shapes, such as bridge, tower, house.

Plenary

Before the end of the lesson, bring all the groups together and look at the lesson word wall. Ask the children what an irregular verb is. They should say '*A verb that changes its spelling when it describes a past action.*'

Support

Help children who need support in recognising irregular verbs by creating a little word wall of irregular verbs for their own use. They can colour code the words. In a literacy time, spend some time looking at a couple of the irregular verbs and use rhymes or pictures to reinforce them. *The cat sits on the mat, the cat sat on the mat.*

Extension

Encourage the children to build up irregular verb word banks and to use them to create poems, recounts or narratives. Ask the children if they can see any patterns in some of the irregular spellings, for example, verbs ending with '-w' such as *draw, blow, know, grow,* have '-ew' at end of irregular past tense verbs – *drew, blew, knew, grew.*

Irregular verbs pairs

see

go

eat

come

sit

fall

Irregular verbs pairs

say

win

do

give

grow

draw

Irregular verbs pairs

saw

went

ate

came

sat

fell

Irregular verbs pairs

said

won

did

gave

grew

drew

Irregular verbs wall

Name _____

Verbs that have different spellings when they are describing past actions are called irregular verbs.

The past tense irregular verbs are missing in this word wall.
Write them next to their correct pair, see – saw.

see			tell	

dig		run		fall	

go		get		do	

make		come		sit	

saw	went	came	dug	did	fell	got	made	ran	sat	told

Complete these sentences using words from the word wall above.

The dog _____ up a juicy bone.

I will _____ up this treasure chest.

Ouch! I _____ out of the tree.

Look at how the snowflakes _____.

Mum says I can _____ to the cinema.

Dad and I _____ to the football match.

Becky _____ down on the chair.

Thea wants to _____ on the floor.

Chapter 4 – Adjectives

Adjective information

Adjectives	Adjectives are words which describe or tell us more about a noun. Adjectives can make sentences more interesting. We can use more than one adjective together in one sentence – *the tall, white mountains stood in front of them.*		
	Adjectives can go before a noun.		*The furry cat purred.*
	Adjectives can go after a noun.		*The house was very spooky.*
Types of adjective	**Descriptive adjectives**	Describe people, places, animals and objects.	*The happy dragon flew into the clear sky. The round orange smelt delicious.*
	Number adjectives	Describe how many there are of a noun.	*one man, two dogs, eighty doors*
	Colour adjectives	Describe the colour of a noun.	*white hair, orange face, yellow moon, red nose, blue trousers*
	Shape adjectives	Describe the shape of a noun.	*The round moon shone like a glistening diamond. The boy nervously picked up the square tin.*
	Adjectives made from suffixes '-ful', '-less'	Adjectives can sometimes be made by the attachment use of suffixes to verbs and nouns. Add the suffix onto the end of the root word.	*careless, careful, hopeless, hopeful*
		If the root word has more than one syllable and ends in '-y' with a consonant before it, change the '-y' to '-i' and then add the suffixes.	*beauty – beautiful penny – penniless*
	Making adverbs by adding '-ly' to adjectives.	Adverbs (words used to describe verbs) can be made by adding the suffix '-ly' to adjectives.	*sad – sadly poor – poorly hopeful – hopefully*
		If the root word has more than one syllable and ends in '-y' with a consonant before it, change the '-y' to '- i' and then add the suffixes.	*happy – happily merry – merrily*
	Changing adjective meanings using the prefix 'un-'	The prefix 'un-' can be added to the front of some adjectives to describe the opposite meaning (an antonym).	*kind – unkind wise – unwise*

Adjective information continued

Grading scale of adjectives	Absolute adjectives	Basic adjectives that describe a noun.		Bob has a new camera.
	Comparative adjectives	Comparative adjectives are adjectives that compare one noun with another. Rule: for most comparative adjectives add '-er'.		Bob has got a newer camera than Millie.
		When the root adjective ends in '-y' with a consonant before it, change the '-y' to '-i' and then add '-er'.		busy – busier
	Superlative adjectives	Adjectives that describe a noun of the highest quality or ability. Rule: for most superlative adjectives add '-est'.		Bob has got the newest camera.
		When the root adjective ends in '-y' with a consonant before it, then change the '-y' to '-i' and then add '-est'.		busy – busiest
	Root		Comparative	Superlative
	long		longer	longest
	big		bigger	biggest
	busy		busier	busiest

Adjective objective chart

Objectives and year group	Descriptive adjectives	Changing adjectives with 'un-' prefix	Making adjectives with suffixes (Year 2)	Uses of suffixes '-er' and '-est' (Year 2)
Word – Year 1				
Recognise adjectives.	★	★	★	★
How the pre-fix 'un-' changes the meaning of adjectives.		★		
Word – Year 2				
Use adjectives.	★	★	★	★
Formation of adjectives using suffixes such as '-ful', '-less'.			★	
Use of suffixes '-er', '-est' in adjectives.				★
Use of '-ly' to turn adjectives into adverbs.			★	
Sentence – Year 1				
How words can combine to make sentences.	★	★	★	★
Sentence – Year 2				
Different sentences, statement, question, exclamation, command.	★	★	★	★
Text – Year 1				
Sequencing sentences to form short narrative.	★	★	★	
Text – Year 2				
Use of present and past tense in writing.		★	★	

Adjective springboards

Who am I?

Put the children into groups. Give them each a story character that all the children know. Ask each group to come up and use adjectives to describe the character, for example 'This character is young. She is very kind and helpful.' The other children have to try and guess who it is after each descriptive sentence.

Adjective displays

With the children create pictures of different settings from a story that the children will know or could be studying as a class. Give each group a setting to draw or paint. Put the settings in order of the story and encourage the children to use adjectives to describe each one. Write adjective labels to go with the pictures.

The children could work in groups to make different story settings, such as a space setting, a fantasy fairy tale setting, an everyday street or school setting, a haunted house setting.

Once they are displayed, encourage the children to create adjective labels for their pictures.

Do the above activity with a story character or types of story characters. Encourage the children to create captions to describe the characters' clothes and the characters' personalities.

Give each child a picture of a person, animal, a place or an object. Give out 'The word web' (See Teacher resources on CD-ROM) and ask the children to write down all the adjectives they can think of to describe the picture.

Ask the children to create their own story character, Let them draw a picture and use given or adjectives of their choice to write about it.

Word walls

Create eye catching word walls. One flash card equals one brick. Have several bricks to create the word wall with the children. Have blank cards that the children can write new nouns and add to or make a new word wall shape.

They can be used in a variety of ways:

• Adjectives for different settings/characters looks and personalities/objects

• Antonym pair

• Synonym words.

The word ladder

A similar game to 'Consequences'. In groups of four the children are given strips of paper with four sections (see Word ladder Template – Teacher resources). The children write a adjective on the first section, fold over the paper to hide it and pass it to the next child. They then write another adjective on the next and so on. After the strip has been completed it is opened up and the children read out the four written adjectives.

The children use the adjectives to describe a place, a character or an object to the rest of the children. They could also draw a picture using the adjectives.

Word wheel/ Word slide

(see Teacher resources for templates)
The teacher or children add nouns to the wheels or slides to explore and discover other words such as synonyms and antonyms. Also a good reinforcement resource.

Other ideas

• Bingo – antonyms.

• Pairs – antonyms.

• Creating and working out word searches.

• Using the star puzzle template for a quiz.

• Creating alliterative sentences using adjectives, for example The big bear bounced over the brown rock.

• Alphabet adjectives.

• Synonyms mobiles for a word such as snow/cold – could be icicles hanging down with the word on it, rain drops with words etc.

• Bring in an object such as a pumpkin or an orange and ask the children to use five senses to describe it.

Descriptive adjectives 1 – settings

Learning objectives

- To understand that adjectives are words that describe nouns.

- To understand that adjectives can help you imagine what something looks like.

- To recognise and use simple adjectives to describe places and objects.

Resources

- **Lesson** – An interesting object e.g. fruit or vegetable, unusual shaped teapot etc. Pictures/paintings/photographs.

- **Group 1 (Year 1)** – Blank paper for drawing, pencils and colouring pencils, pen and card or paper labels.

- **Group 2 (Year 1/2)** – Copies of activity sheet 1 'Describing objects' for each child. Blank paper, pencils and colouring pencils. Story books.

- **Group 3 (Year 2)** – Copies of activity sheet 3 'Adjectives for a fantasy world.' for each child. Story books.

Lesson/activity notes

- **Lesson** – The internet usually has a good range of pictures/photos that could be shown to the class via a large computer screen.

- **Group 1 (Year 1)** – Children work individually and then as a discussion group with adult support.

- **Group 2 (Year 1/2)** – Children work as a discussion group with an adult and then individually.

- **Group 3 (Year 2)** – Children work as a discussion group, then individually and finally pair-sharing their work.

Lesson

Introduction

Bring in an interesting object such as a vegetable or an unusual shaped pot. Ask children what it looks like. Write their describing words on a whiteboard. Explain that the words are called adjectives and are used to describe nouns – places, objects, people, creatures. Highlight how adjectives can make writing and reading more interesting. Give them contrasting sentences as an example, *'Kelvin picked up the teapot'* to *'Kelvin picked up the round teapot with yellow spots'*.

Main lesson

Highlight that adjectives can help readers imagine what or a place looks like. Display a picture, or photograph of a distinct place, e.g. a snowy setting, a lush rainforest, a fantasy or a space setting. Ask the children to look closely at the scene and the objects within it – mountains, trees, buildings. Encourage the children to think of adjectives to describe the nouns in the setting and write them next to the picture. Work with the children to create sentences describing the setting.

Explain to the children that they are going to do activities using adjectives to describe story settings. Put the children into their levelled groups and give out the activities. Spend time moving between the groups to discuss individual children's work and assess their level of understanding.

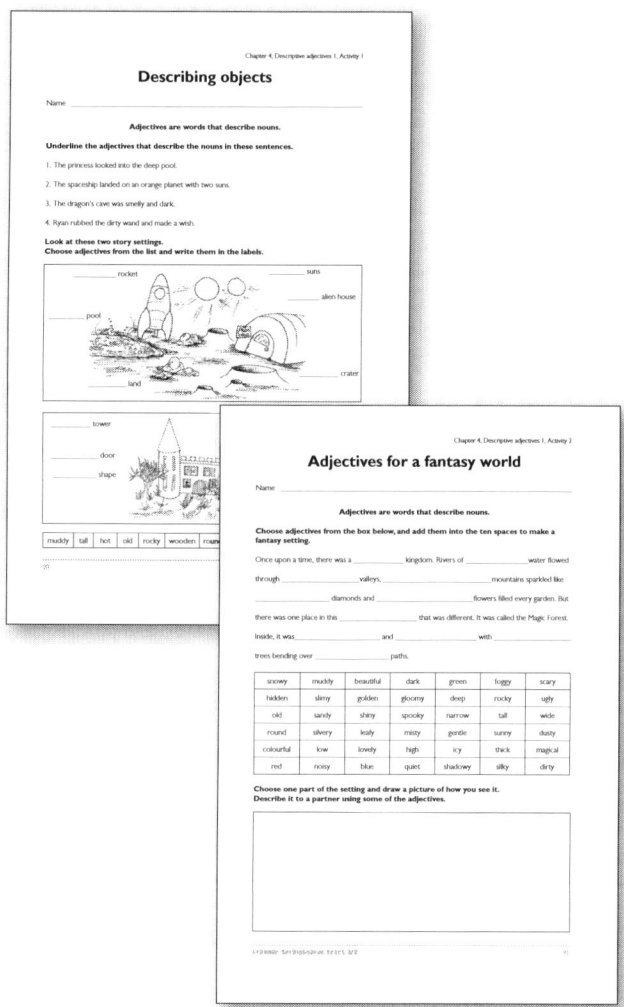

Activities

Group 1 (Year 1)

- Give the children a choice of fantasy story settings, let them choose their own, for example an alien garden, a dragon's cave, a magic wood, a school or town in the future, an ogre's castle.

- Ask them to draw and colour their story setting on the blank paper.

- Once the children have completed their drawings, ask each child what adjectives they would use to describe the nouns in their setting.

- Write the adjectives down on the card or paper labels.

- Ask the rest of the children for other adjectives that could be used and write them out.

- Display their work with the adjective word labels around each setting picture.

Group 2 (Year 1/2)
- With the children as a group, discuss how adjectives can help describe imaginary worlds by looking at examples in a few stories and books.

- Give out the copies of 'Describing objects' to each child.

- The children then match the adjectives to two story setting pictures by writing them in the correct boxes under the right pictures.

- On a separate piece of paper, the children draw their own story setting and write adjectives underneath their picture.

Group 3 (Year 2)
- With the children as a group, discuss how adjectives can help describe imaginary worlds by looking at examples in a few stories and books.

- Give the copies of 'Adjectives for a fantasy world' to each child.

- Working individually, the children add adjectives to complete a short passage.

- They then draw their own fantasy setting from a choice of adjectives, circling the ones they used.

- Once they have completed the drawings, ask the children to pair–share their work.

- Encourage them to think of other adjectives they could add to the picture.

Plenary
Before the end of the lesson, bring the groups together. Discuss their setting pictures and the adjectives used to describe the nouns in the settings. Highlight that adjectives can make writing more fun and interesting and help readers imagine places and objects more clearly.

Support
Use the senses to help children use adjectives to describe objects. Bring in fruit, vegetables or flowers to show to the children. Ask them to use the senses to describe the object, smell = sweet, feels = slimy, looks = red, sounds = crunchy.

Extension
Make a pile of adjective cards and put them in a pile in front of the children. Let the children take turns to pick an adjective and then use a small whiteboard or paper to write a sentence using the chosen adjective. Increase the number of adjective cards per sentence as they get more able.

Describing objects

Name _____

Adjectives are words that describe nouns.

Underline the adjectives that describe the nouns in these sentences.

1. The princess looked into the deep pool.

2. The spaceship landed on an orange planet with two suns.

3. The dragon's cave was smelly and dark.

4. Ryan rubbed the dirty wand and made a wish.

Look at these two story settings.
Choose adjectives from the list and write them in the labels.

| muddy | tall | hot | old | rocky | wooden | round | high | two | spooky | wide | square |

Adjectives for a fantasy world

Name _____

Adjectives are words that describe nouns.

Choose adjectives from the box below, and add them into the ten spaces to make a fantasy setting.

Once upon a time, there was a _____ kingdom. Rivers of _____ water flowed

through _____ valleys, _____ mountains sparkled like

_____ diamonds and _____ flowers filled every garden. But

there was one place in this _____ that was different. It was called the Magic Forest.

Inside, it was _____ and _____ with _____

trees bending over _____ paths.

snowy	muddy	beautiful	dark	green	foggy	scary
hidden	slimy	golden	gloomy	deep	rocky	ugly
old	sandy	shiny	spooky	narrow	tall	wide
round	silvery	leafy	misty	gentle	sunny	dusty
colourful	low	lovely	high	icy	thick	magical
red	noisy	blue	quiet	shadowy	silky	dirty

**Choose one part of the setting and draw a picture of how you see it.
Describe it to a partner using some of the adjectives.**

Descriptive adjectives 2 – people

Learning objectives

- To understand that adjectives are words that tell us more about nouns.

- To understand that adjectives can help you imagine what someone looks like.

- To recognise and use simple adjectives to describe people or creatures.

Resources

- **Lesson** – Story character picture – Pictures or photos of a variety of creatures, such as animals, birds, mini–beasts, reptiles, sea–life.

- **Group 1 (Year 1)** – Copies of activity sheet 1 'Describing story characters' and activity sheet 1.2 'My story character' for each child. .

- **Group 2 (Year 1/2)** – Copies of activity sheet 2 'Wanted!' for each child. Pencils, colouring pencils, (Lesson resources CD-ROM).

- **Group 3 (Year 2)** – Copies of activity sheet 3 'Describing a story character'. Pencils, colouring pencils, (Lesson resources CD-ROM).

Lesson/activity notes

- **Group 1 (Year 1)** – Children work individually on their activity sheet with adult support.

- **Group 2 (Year 1/2)** – Children work individually on their activity sheet and as a group playing 'Adjective consequences'.

- **Group 3 (Year 2)** – Children work individually on their activity sheet and as a group playing 'Adjective consequences'.

Lesson

Introduction

Show the picture of the story character to the children. Ask them to think of words to describe the character. Write the words around the character. Highlight that these words are called adjectives. Highlight how adjectives can make story characters more interesting or describe their special features.

Main lesson

Explain that adjectives can give a lot of information. They can be numbers, colour, size, shape, moods. Draw a table on the white board with subtitles – Colour, Number, Size, Shape, Touch. Put the children into groups of two or three

and give each group a photograph or picture of creature to study, such as elephant, cat, parrot, octopus, spider, snake. In turn ask each group to give you adjectives for each heading to describe their creature and write them in the table, for example one trunk, wrinkly skin, slimy skin. Underline the adjectives.

Explain to the children that they are going to work in groups to do activities using adjectives to describe story characters. Put the children into their levelled groups and give out the activities. Spend time moving between the groups to discuss individual children's work and assess their level of understanding.

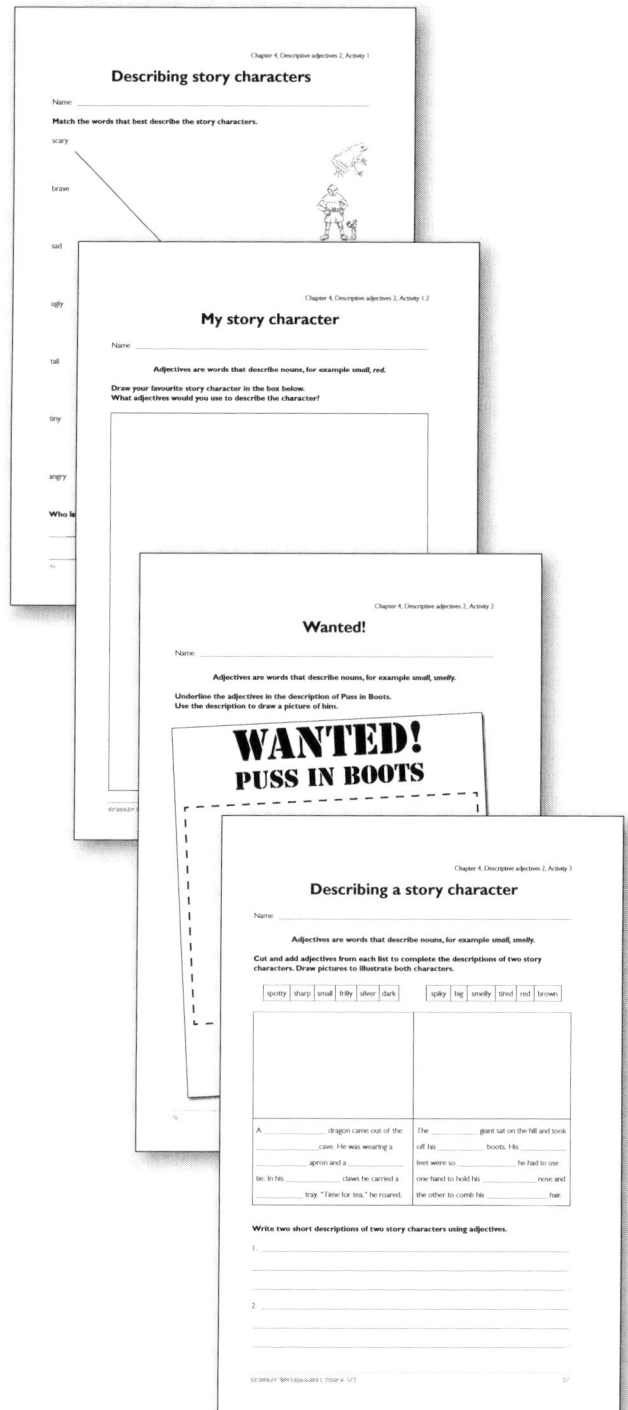

Activities

Group 1

- Give the children copies of activity sheet 1 'Describing story characters'.

- With the children, discuss the different pictures of the story characters. Encourage children to describe each character concerning their size, how they are feeling, their looks.

- Read through the adjective words and explain that they are used to describe nouns like people. The children then draw lines from the words to the character that they best describe.

- Encourage the children to say a sentence for each picture and adjective, for example: the scary dragon roared loudly.

- Read out the question at the end of the sheet and have a discussion on the children's favourite story character. Can they describe them well? Give them each a copy of 'My story character' to draw their story character.

Group 2 (Year 1/2)

- Give copies of activity sheet 2, 'Wanted!' to each child.

- The children then underline the adjectives of a description of well known story character on 'Wanted' poster.

- The children can then draw a picture of the character and add the character's name on the poster – Puss in Boots.

- Discuss with the children how the adjectives give the reader a clearer picture of the character.

Group 3 (Year 2)

- Give the children copies of the activity sheet 3, 'Describing a story character,'

- Working individually, the children add adjectives from a list to describe two story characters and then draw pictures to illustrate the characters.

- Then they write two short descriptions to describe two of their own story characters.

- Encourage the children to share their descriptions and discuss how adjectives can give a clearer picture of a character.

Plenary

Before the end of the lesson, bring the groups together. Ask the children about the characters that they have created or described in their activities. Remind the children how adjectives can make their writing more fun and interesting and help readers imagine story characters more clearly.

Support

Use drama and role play to help children use adjectives. Put them on a hot–seat and ask them to describe a fellow character and their personality. Look at good and bad characters. Write down the adjectives so that they can be used as a word bank for the children.

Extension

Encourage the children to look at a variety of fictional, non-fictional and poetry texts for examples of adjectives that describe people and creatures. Suggest they create a word bank to collect adjective examples.

Describing story characters

Name _____

Match the words that best describe the story characters.

scary

brave

sad

ugly

tall

tiny

angry

Who is your favourite story character? What are they like?

_____

My story character

Name _____

Adjectives are words that describe nouns, for example *small, red*.

Draw your favourite story character in the box below.
What adjectives would you use to describe the character?

Wanted!

Name _____

Adjectives are words that describe nouns, for example *small, smelly.*

Underline the adjectives in the description of Puss in Boots.
Use the description to draw a picture of him.

WANTED!
PUSS IN BOOTS

Have you seen a black and white cat?
He has blue eyes and long whiskers.
He walks on his two back paws.
He has large boots and a smart, green jacket.
He has a big hat with a white feather.

Describing a story character

Name _____

Adjectives are words that describe nouns, for example *small, smelly*.

Cut and add adjectives from each list to complete the descriptions of two story characters. Draw pictures to illustrate both characters.

spotty	sharp	small	frilly	silver	dark

spiky	big	smelly	tired	red	brown

A _____ dragon came out of the _____cave. He was wearing a _____ apron and a _____ tie. In his _____ claws he carried a _____ tray. "Time for tea," he roared.

The _____ giant sat on the hill and took off his _____ boots. His _____ feet were so _____ he had to use one hand to hold his _____ nose and the other to comb his _____ hair.

Write two short descriptions of two story characters using adjectives.

1. _____

_____

_____ .

2. _____

_____

_____ .

Changing adjectives with prefix 'un-'

Learning objectives
- To understand what a prefix means.

- To understand how the prefix 'un-' can change the meaning of adjectives.

- To discover the types of adjectives that can have the 'un-' prefix.

Resources
- **Lesson** – Board or paper for writing.

- **Group 1 (Year 1)** – Cut up cards from the activity sheet 1, 'Matching game with 'un-' prefixes' for each child or a couple of sets for a pair of children.

- **Group 2 (Year 1/2)** – Cut up cards from the activity sheet 1, 'Matching game with 'un-' prefixes' for each child or a couple of sets for a pair of children.

- **Group 3 (Year 2)** – Copies of activity sheet 2, 'Opposite adjectives using prefix 'un-'' for each child.

Lesson/activity notes
- **Lesson** – In a discussion group.

- **Group 1 (Year 1)** – Children work individually or in pairs with adult support.

- **Group 2 (Year 1/2)** – Children work in pairs or individually.

- **Group 3 (Year 2)** – Children work individually.

Lesson

Introduction
Remind the children what an adjective is. Explain how some adjectives can change their meaning by adding a set of short words in front of them. Explain that these short words are called prefixes. Introduce the prefix 'un-' and say the sound. Let the children say the sound of the prefix after you. If you have already done the lesson on 'un-' prefixes for verbs, you may want to remind the children of how the prefix changed the verbs.

Main lesson
Write the adjective words *happy* and *kind*. Ask the children to help you write out two sentences using both words in it. Explain that you are now going to add the prefix to the two adjectives – *unhappy* and *unkind*.

Ask the children what happens when the 'un-' is put in front of the words (they have opposite meanings). Highlight how they are negative meanings. With the

children's help write sentences using *unhappy* and *unkind*. Encourage the children to help you list other 'un-' adjective words. Check that they are not using verbs. Explain that they will be doing activities to discover more about using the 'un-' prefix in front of adjectives.

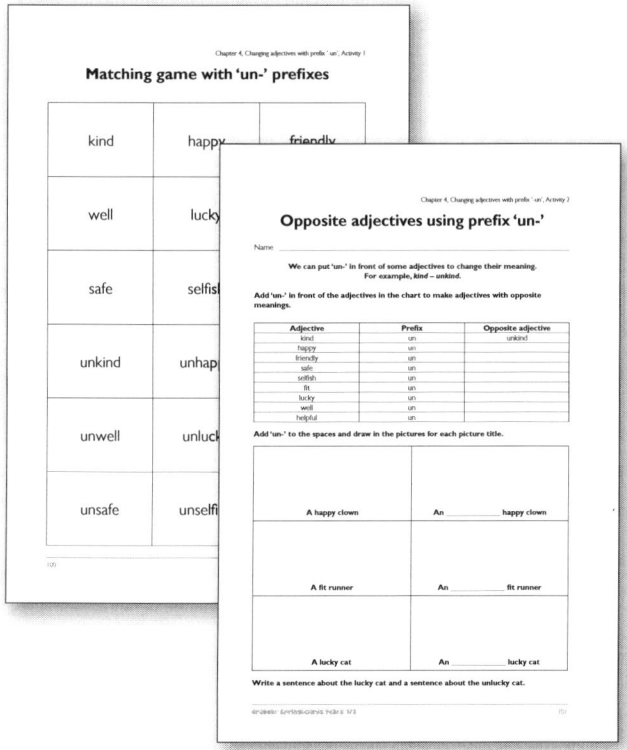

Activities

Group 1
- Have the children in a small group or in pairs.

- Use the cards to play various games, such as matching pairs where the children put the pair cards together, or they lay out the adjective cards and use a pile of prefix

- 'un-' cards to place on top.

- Let the children choose one pair of adjectives (with prefix and without) and orally describe examples of the adjectives in simple sentences.

- Discuss how the 'un-' prefix gives the adjectives their opposite meanings. Allow the children to think of other examples.

Group 2 (Year 1/2)
- Put the children in pairs and give them a pile of adjective cards and a pile of prefix adjective cards.

- Ask the pairs to play a matching snap style game.

- They then choose a pair of adjectives. Ask them to say sentences using them and then they can write their sentences out.

Grammar Springboards Years 1/2

- Encourage the pair to share their sentences with other pairs. Ask – *Can you think of other adjectives that can have a prefix in front of them?* Let the children list their words.

Group 3 (Year 2)

- Give out the copies of 'Opposite adjectives using prefix 'un-'' to each child.

- Working individually, the children add the prefix to a chart of adjectives. Before they move to the next exercise, let the children discuss the different meanings of each adjective and their prefix. Note how they are totally opposite in meaning.

- They then add the prefix to six captions and draw pictures to illustrate the opposites.

- Finally, they write a sentence about a lucky cat and another sentence about an unlucky cat. Let them pair-share their work.

Plenary

Ten minutes before the end of the lesson, bring all the children together. Let them share their work with each other. Remind the children what a prefix is and how 'un-' can give the opposite descriptive words for certain adjectives.

Support

Let the children draw pictures to illustrate the changes in the adjectives when 'un-' is added. They can have one drawing for the positive adjective and one drawing for the negative adjective. Encourage them to label the drawings with the words.

Extension

Encourage the children to create a word bank of adjectives that can have the 'un-' prefix in front of it.

Matching game with 'un-' prefixes

kind	happy	friendly
well	lucky	helpful
safe	selfish	fit
unkind	unhappy	unfriendly
unwell	unlucky	unhelpful
unsafe	unselfish	unfit

Opposite adjectives using prefix 'un-'

Name _____

**We can put 'un-' in front of some adjectives to change their meaning.
For example, *kind – unkind*.**

Add 'un-' in front of the adjectives in the chart to make adjectives with opposite meanings.

Adjective	Prefix	Opposite adjective
kind	un	unkind
happy	un	
friendly	un	
safe	un	
selfish	un	
fit	un	
lucky	un	
well	un	
helpful	un	

Add 'un-' to the spaces and draw in the pictures for each picture title.

A happy clown	**An _____ happy clown**
A fit runner	**An _____ fit runner**
A lucky cat	**An _____ lucky cat**

Write a sentence about the lucky cat and a sentence about the unlucky cat.

Making adjectives with suffixes '-ful' and '-less'

Learning objectives
- To understand what a suffix is.

- To investigate making adjectives with the suffixes '-ful' and '-less'.

- To create adjectives using the suffixes '-ful' and '-less'.

Resources
- **Group 1 (Year 1)** – Cut up cards from the activity sheet 1 for each child or pair of children. Blank card or paper and pens.

- **Group 2 (Year 1/2)** – Copies of activity sheet 2 'Floating adjectives' for each child.

- **Group 3 (Year 2)** – Copies of activity sheet 3 'Opposite adjectives from '-ful' and '-less'' for each child.

Lesson/activity notes
- **Lesson** – In a discussion group.

- **Group 1 (Year 1)** – Children work individually or in pairs with adult support.

- **Group 2 (Year 1/2)** – Children work in pairs or individually.

- **Group 3 (Year 2)** – Children work individually.

Do the same routine with the suffix '-less' and once again highlight the '-y' rule for any root words that end in '-y'. Explain to the children that they are going to work on activities to do with the suffixes '–ful' and '-less'.

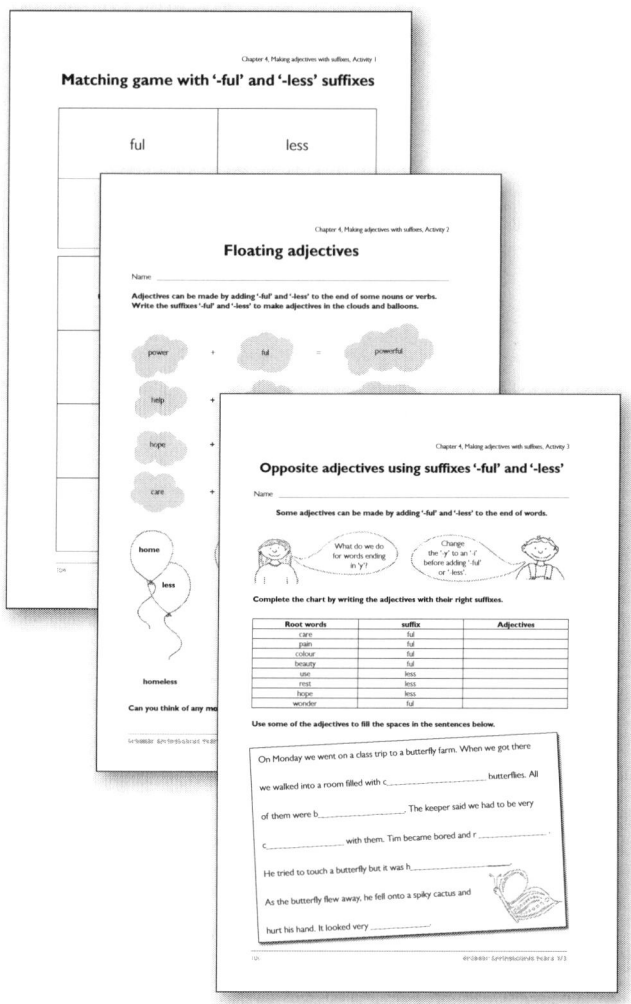

Lesson

Introduction
Remind the children what an adjective is – a word that describes a noun. Explain that sets of small letters called suffixes can be added to the end of some nouns and verbs to make new adjectives.

Main lesson
Write the suffixes '-ful' and '-less' for the children to see. Introduce them as suffixes that work magic on some verbs and nouns by turning them into adjectives.

Say an example for the suffix '-ful' such as care '-ful'. Write the word on the board and underline the root word in one colour and the suffix in another. Orally make a sentence up using the word 'care-ful'. Ask the children if they can think of any other words ending with '-ful' and list them on the board, underlining the suffix each time.

Highlight or write out the adjective – beauti-ful'. Explain that the root word is the noun 'beauty'. Show how the '-y' is replaced by an '-i' before the suffix.

Activities

Group 1
- Have the children in a small group or in pairs.

- Use the cards to create adjective making sums with the children. Put out a root word and then the + sign. Ask the children what suffix they could add on to make an adjective.

- Let them work out the adjective by saying the word. Complete the sum by adding = and the suffix . Write out the adjective sum on blank card or paper.

- Continue creating more adjective making sums.

- Once all the root cards have been turned into adjectives, let the children read them out.

Group 2 (Year 1/2)
- Give out the copies of 'Floating adjectives' to each child.

- Highlight the information and example at the top of the sheet. The children then make adjectives by adding the suffix '-ful' to the end of three words.

- They then do the same by adding the suffix '-less' to the end of three words.

- Let the children discuss what other adjectives they can think of that end in '-ful' and '-less' and write the words down.

Group 3 (Year 2)
- Give out the copies of 'Opposite adjectives using suffixes '-ful' and '-less'' to each child.

- Highlight the information and rules at the top of the sheet.

- Working individually, the children complete a chart by writing the adjectives with the right suffixes and spellings.

- They then use some of the adjectives to fill in the missing gaps in a class journal text.

- Encourage the children to share their work.

Plenary
Ten minutes before the end of the lesson, bring all the children together to share their work. Go over what is a suffix and the spelling rules related to some of the words. Highlight how the adjectives make their writing more interesting.

Support
Encourage the children to orally use some of the adjectives in a short story. Let them record the story or have someone act as a scribe.

Extension
Encourage the children to create short stories using some of the adjectives with the '-ful' and '-less' suffixes. How many can they use?

Matching game with '-ful' and '-less' suffixes

ful	less
+	=

care	pain	help
play	wonder	joy
rest	home	hope
use	hair	power

Floating adjectives

Name _____

Adjectives can be made by adding '-ful' and '-less' to the end of some nouns or verbs. Write the suffixes '-ful' and '-less' to make adjectives in the clouds and balloons.

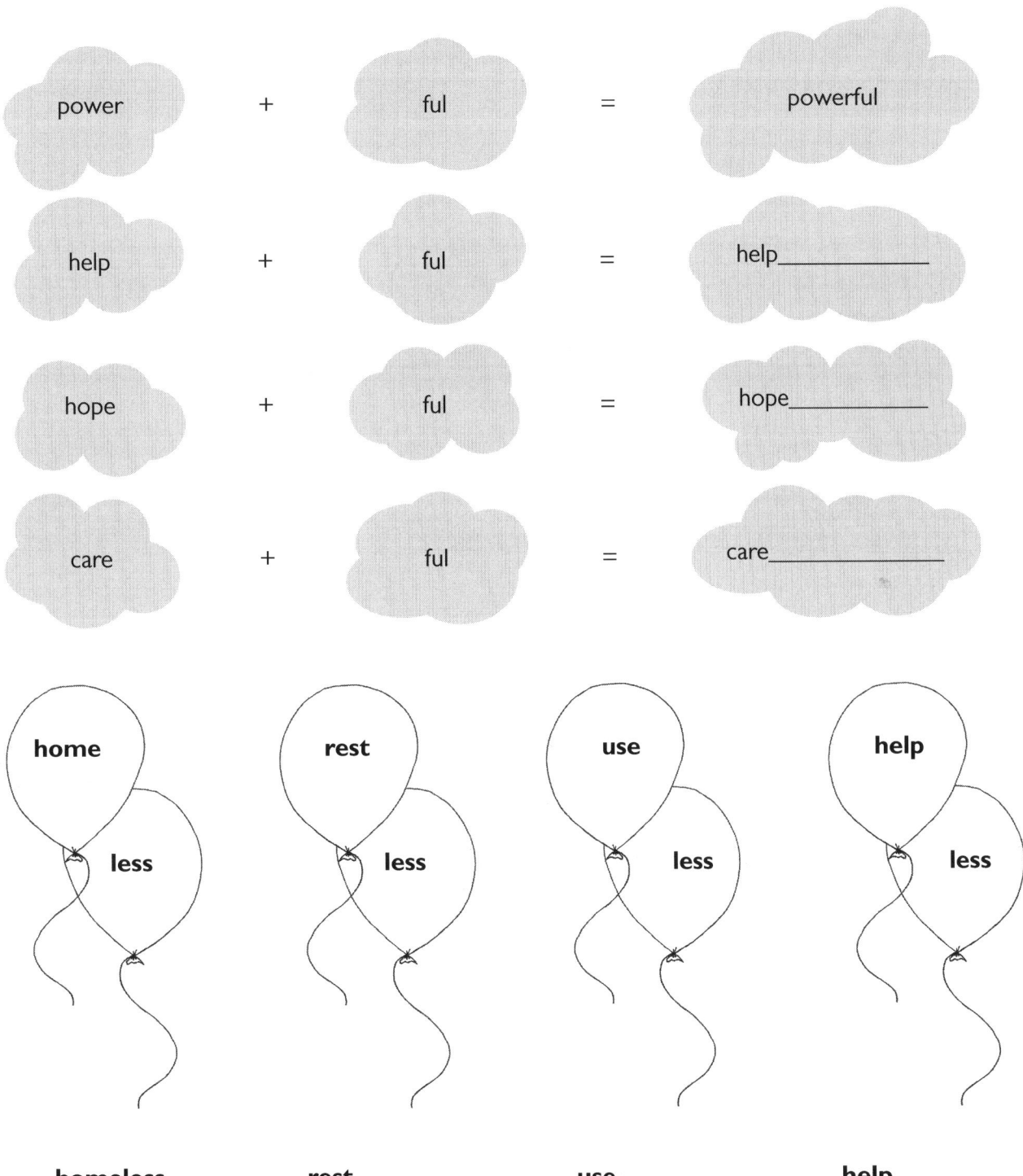

power + ful = powerful

help + ful = help_____

hope + ful = hope_____

care + ful = care_____

home   less   homeless

rest   less   rest_____

use   less   use_____

help   less   help_____

Can you think of any more words ending in '-ful' or '-less'?

Opposite adjectives using suffixes '-ful' and '-less'

Name _____

Some adjectives can be made by adding '-ful' and '-less' to the end of words.

What do we do for words ending in 'y'?

Change the '-y' to an '-i' before adding '-ful' or '-less'.

Complete the chart by writing the adjectives with their right suffixes.

Root words	suffix	Adjectives
care	ful	
pain	ful	
colour	ful	
beauty	ful	
use	less	
rest	less	
hope	less	
wonder	ful	

Use some of the adjectives to fill the spaces in the sentences below.

On Monday we went on a class trip to a butterfly farm. When we got there

we walked into a room filled with c_____ butterflies. All

of them were b_____. The keeper said we had to be very

c_____ with them. Tim became bored and r_____.

He tried to touch a butterfly but it was h_____.

As the butterfly flew away, he fell onto a spiky cactus and

hurt his hand. It looked very _____.

Making adverbs from adjectives using '-ly'

Learning objectives
- To understand what adverbs and adjectives are.

- To understand how adverbs can be made by adding '-ly' to adjectives.

- To make '-ly' adverbs and use them in writing.

Resources
- **Lesson** – Board or paper.

- **Group 1 (Year 1)** – Copies of activity sheet 1, 'Adjectives to adverbs using '-ly'' for each child.

- **Group 2 (Year 1/2)** – Copies of activity sheet 2, 'Making adverbs using suffix '-ly'' for each child.

- **Group 3 (Year 2)** – Copies of activity sheet 3, 'Adjectives to adverbs using '-ly'' for each child.

Lesson/activity notes
- **Lesson** – As a discussion group and in pairs for a drama session.

- **Group 1 (Year 1)** – Children work in pairs with adult support.

- **Group 2 (Year 1/2)** – Children work individually.

- **Group 3 (Year 2)** – Children work individually and pair-share their work.

guess what the adverb is and the verb it is describing? Explain to the children that they will be doing activities looking at using '–ly' adverbs in writing.

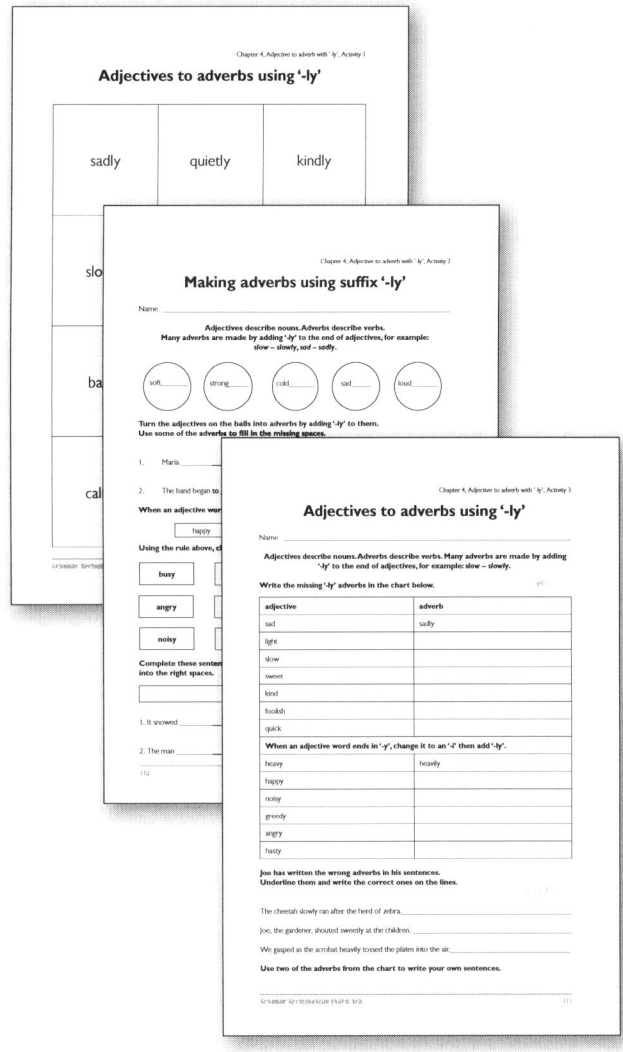

Lesson

Introduction
Remind the children how adjectives describe nouns. Give an example such as '*the slow tortoise*'. Introduce adverbs. Explain that an adverb describes verbs – how an action is done. Say an example, such as '*The tortoise walked slowly*.' Highlight the verb walked and explain that slowly helps the reader know how the tortoise walked.

Explain that they are going to find out how one suffix can turn some adjectives into adverbs.

Main lesson
Write '-ly' for all the children to see and say the sound. Let the children say the sound after you.

Write the word '*slow*' and say it. Add the '-ly' and say the word – '*slowly*'. With support, let the children suggest other examples of adverbs with '-ly' such as loudly, quietly, and quickly. Put the children in pairs and ask them to act out an '-ly' adverb to the others in the group. Can they

Activities

Group 1
- Give out the copies of 'Adjectives to adverbs using '-ly' to each child or a pair of children.

- Point to the three words with the underlined '-ly' at the top of the chart and ask the children to read the words out.

- Remind the children that the words are adverbs which describe verbs and actions. Ask them to say sentences using the adverbs.

- Now ask them to say the words without the '-ly' sound – sad, quiet, kind. Remind the children that the words are now adjectives and describe nouns. Let them say sentences using the adjectives.

- Let them continue with a partner to choose more adverb words and to use them in sentences.

Group 2 (Year 1/2)

- Give out the copies of 'Making adverbs using suffix '-ly'' to each child and ask them to read the information at the top of the sheet.

- Working individually, the children add the suffix '-ly' to a set of adjectives to make them adverbs. They then use three of the adverbs to fill the spaces in three sentences.

- After reading the rule on changing '-y' to '-i' for using '-ly', the children use the rule to help them change the adjectives that end in '-y' into '-ly' adverbs.

- Finally they add the right '-ly' adverbs into sentences from a list of adjectives.

- Once they have completed the activity, check the children understand how the adverbs describe the verbs and why they are important in descriptive writing.

Group 3 (Year 2)

- Give out the copies of 'Adjectives to adverbs using '-ly'' to each child and ask them to read the information at the top of the sheet.

- Working individually, the children complete a chart by turning lists of adjectives into adverbs using the suffix '-ly'.

- They then read sentences in which the wrong '-ly' adverb has been used. At the end of the sentence they add an '-ly' adverb that they think is more suitable for the sentences.

- Finally, they use two of the adverbs from the chart to create their own sentences. Encourage the children to say their sentences before they write them out. Let them pair-share their work.

Plenary

Ten minutes before the end of the lesson, bring all the children together to share their work. Remind the children that adverbs describe verbs and their actions.

Support

Help the children produce a word bank poster of '-ly' adverbs which can be created using a word processor. Have this available in the room for the children to use and read.

Adjectives to adverbs using '-ly'

sadly	quietly	kindly
slowly	loudly	wisely
badly	excitedly	nervously
calmly	beautifully	silently

Making adverbs using suffix '-ly'

Name _____

Adjectives describe nouns. Adverbs describe verbs.
Many adverbs are made by adding '-ly' to the end of adjectives, for example:
slow – slowly, sad – sadly.

soft_____   strong_____   cold_____   sad_____   loud_____

Turn the adjectives on the balls into adverbs by adding '-ly' to them.
Use some of the adverbs to fill in the missing spaces.

1.   Maria _____ stroked the sleeping cat.

2.   The band began to _____ play their music.

When an adjective word ends in '-y', change it to an '-i' then add '-ly'.

| happy | i | ly | happily |

Using the rule above, change these adjectives into '-ly' adverbs.

busy	
angry	
noisy	

Complete these sentences by turning the adjectives into '-ly' adverbs and putting them into the right spaces.

| rude | heavy |

1. It snowed _____ all day.

2. The man _____ pushed in front of the crowd.

Adjectives to adverbs using '-ly'

Name _____

Adjectives describe nouns. Adverbs describe verbs. Many adverbs are made by adding '-ly' to the end of adjectives, for example: *slow – slowly.*

Write the missing '-ly' adverbs in the chart below.

adjective	adverb
sad	sadly
light	
slow	
sweet	
kind	
foolish	
quick	
When an adjective word ends in '-y', change it to an '-i' then add '-ly'.	
heavy	heavily
happy	
noisy	
greedy	
angry	
hasty	

Joe has written the wrong adverbs in his sentences.
Underline them and write the correct ones on the lines.

The cheetah slowly ran after the herd of zebra._____

Joe, the gardener, shouted sweetly at the children. _____

We gasped as the acrobat heavily tossed the plates into the air._____

Use two of the adverbs from the chart to write your own sentences.

Use of suffixes '-er' and '-est'

Learning objectives
- To understand that adjectives can have comparative and superlative forms.

- That we can add the suffixes '-er' and '-est' for comparison.

- To use the adjectives to ask and answer questions about comparisons.

Resources
- **Lesson** – A range of pictures, photographs or objects that show three different sizes or looks.

- **Group 1 (Year 1)** – Copies of activity sheet 1 'Pronoun Tales' for each child.

- **Group 2 (Year 1/2)** – Copies of activity sheet 2, 'Longer or longest?' for each child.

- **Group 3 (Year 2)** – Copies of activity sheet 3, 'Comparing words' for each child.

Lesson/activity notes
- **Lesson** – In a discussion group.

- **Group 1 (Year 1)** – Children work individually and in discussion group with adult support.

- **Group 2 (Year 1/2)** – Children work individually.

- **Group 3 (Year 2)** – Children work individually and pair-share their work.

them to say '*I am cold, I am colder, I am coldest*' while acting the movements of being cold. Write the sentences on the board underlining the suffixes.

Explain to the children that they are going to investigate the suffixes '-er' and '-est' in a set of activities.

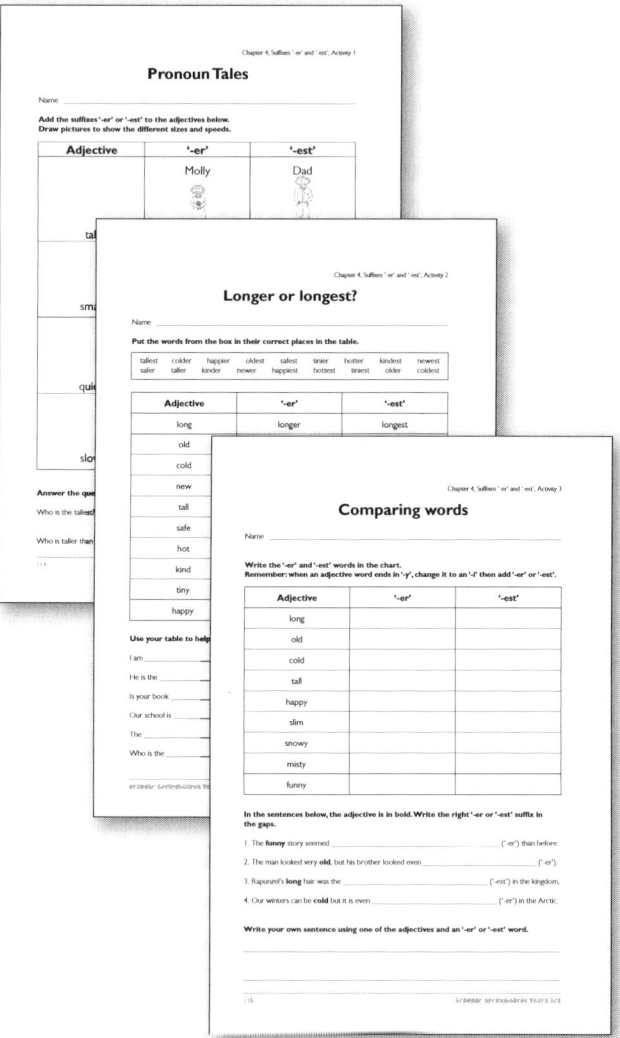

Lesson

Introduction
Show a set of images showing three different sizes of people, animals or objects. Ask the children questions such as: Which is the tallest tower? Is the middle tower taller than the first tower? Which animal is the smallest? Listen to their answers, encouraging contributions from every group.

Main lesson
Introduce the suffixes '-er' and '-est'. Explain that an adjective can show differences in things such as age, looks, size, sound or speed by adding these suffixes.

Write out the adjectives using '-er' and '-est' under the pictures of three examples such as tall, taller and tallest and read them out.

Ask three children to stand up and in order of children, whisper the words – cold, colder and coldest to them. Ask

Activities

Group 1
- Give out the copies of 'Pronoun Tales' to each child.

- In a discussion group, point to the top of the sheet that shows the pictures and words for tall, taller, tallest. Discuss the difference in size and ask questions using the words such as 'Who is tallest?' Who is tall?'

- Read through the other words and let them add the '-er' and '-est' suffixes to the words.

- The children can then draw pictures to show the difference of the comparisons.

- Let the children think of other adjectives they could use with '-er' and '-est', such as loud, louder, loudest.

Group 2 (Year 1/2)

- Give out the copies of 'Longer or longest?' to each child and make sure they understand what to do on the activity sheet.

- Working individually, the children put the right '-er' and '-est' adjectives in their correct places within a chart.

- They then use the adjectives from the chart to complete the sentences.

- Once the children have finished, encourage them to pair-share their answers. Have they differences they need to discuss?

Group 3 (Year 2)

- Give out the copies of 'Comparing words' to each child and make sure they understand what to do on the activity sheet.

- Working individually, the children put the right '-er' and '-est' adjectives in their correct places within a chart.

- They then add the right adjective with either an '-er' or '-est' suffix to complete the sentences.

- Finally, they write their own sentence using an adjective root word and an '-er' or '-est' suffix word.

- Once the children have finished, encourage them to pair-share their answers. Have they differences they need to discuss?

Plenary

Ten minutes before the end of the lesson, bring the children together to share their work and ideas. Finish with an oral game as children compare themselves to another person.

Support

Let the children work with a partner, preparing answers orally before they write them.

Extension

Ask the children to write a fun nonsense poem which has a character or an object being compared in size or sound. Let the children read their poems out to others.

Pronoun Tales

Name _____

Add the suffixes '-er' or '-est' to the adjectives below.
Draw pictures to show the different sizes and speeds.

Adjective	'-er'	'-est'
tall	Molly taller	Dad tallest
small	small_____	small_____
quick	quick_____	quick_____
slow	slow_____	slow_____

Answer the questions.

Who is the tallest? _____

Who is taller than Molly? _____

Longer or longest?

Name _____

Put the words from the box in their correct places in the table.

tallest	colder	happier	oldest	safest	tinier	hotter	kindest	newest
safer	taller	kinder	newer	happiest	hottest	tiniest	older	coldest

Adjective	'-er'	'-est'
long	longer	longest
old		
cold		
new		
tall		
safe		
hot		
kind		
tiny		
happy		

Use your table to help you write answers in the gaps.

I am _____ ('-er') than my best friend.

He is the _____ ('-est') boy in the class.

Is your book _____ ('-er') than mine?

Our school is _____ ('-er') than the school down the road.

The _____ ('-est') place I have visited is Australia.

Who is the _____ ('-est') person you know?

Comparing words

Name _____

Write the '-er' and '-est' words in the chart.
Remember: when an adjective word ends in '-y', change it to an '-i' then add '-er' or '-est'.

Adjective	'-er'	'-est'
long		
old		
cold		
tall		
happy		
slim		
snowy		
misty		
funny		

In the sentences below, the adjective is in bold. Write the right '-er or '-est' suffix in the gaps.

1. The **funny** story seemed _____ ('-er') than before.

2. The man looked very **old**, but his brother looked even _____ ('-er').

3. Rapunzel's **long** hair was the _____ ('-est') in the kingdom.

4. Our winters can be **cold** but it is even _____ ('-er') in the Arctic.

Write your own sentence using one of the adjectives and an '-er' or '-est' word.

_____

_____

Chapter 5 – Sentences

Sentence information

Sentences	Subject of a sentence – what or who the sentence is about. Predicate of a sentence – part of the sentence that does not include the subject, such as the verb.		
	Clause	Main clause – Main part of a sentence.	*I'll make you a cup of tea, after this.*
		Subordinate – It gives more information about the main clause in a sentence.	*Harry felt sick, when he got home.*
Simple sentences	A simple sentence is made up of a subject and a predicate.		*Julia (subject) fell off the see-saw. (Predicate).*
	Sentences begin with a capital letter and finish with a full stop, question mark or an exclamation mark.		
Capital letters	Capital letters are used for a number of reasons:		
	1. At the beginning of a sentence.		*'Today we are going for a walk'.*
	2. For proper nouns.		*Mary, Rose Road, The Three Bears.*
	3. To emphasise certain words in a phrase or sentence.		*'Watch OUT!'*
Compound sentences	A compound sentence is made from two simple sentences joined together by a conjunction.		
Conjunctions – joining words	Conjunctions are words that link words and sentences.		
	Co-ordinating conjunctions. Phrases or words that are equal in information. Both main clauses can be linked into one sentence by using co-ordinating conjunction words such as and, or, but.		*I like pasta <u>but</u> I don't like rice.* *Leo is upstairs <u>and</u> I am downstairs.*
	Subordination conjunctions. A main clause and subordinate clause (minor clause) that are unequal can be joined into one sentence by using subordinate conjunctions such as when, if, that, because.		*My nan is cooking tea <u>when</u> she is back.* *I have a sore arm <u>because</u> I fell over.*
Time connectives	Time connectives are words and phrases used in sentences to highlight the time of the main subject – first, then , next, later, tomorrow, just then, afterwards.		*I will do my homework in a <u>minute</u>. <u>First</u> I must have a biscuit.*
Prepositions	Prepositions are connective words that describe where someone or something is within a sentence – under, above, on, behind, below. A preposition is usually before the noun.		*The man sat <u>on</u> the bench. I put the duvet <u>over</u> my head.*
Complex sentences	A complex sentence consists of a main clause with one or more subordinate clauses.		*<u>Although</u> it was difficult, I enjoyed making the cake.*
Sentence structure	1. Declarative (for statements and suggestions).		*The snow is melting. Maybe the children could go out later.*
	2. Interrogative (for questions and requests).		*When will the playground be clear? Will you check the steps?*
	3. Imperative (for commands and instructions).		*Stop sliding! Take the next turning right.*
	4. Exclamative (for exclamations).		*How peaceful she looks! What a shame!*

Sentence objective chart

Objectives and year group	Simple sentences	Joining words (co-ordination) Year 2	Joining words (subordination) Year 2	Simple time connectives
Sentence – Year 1				
How words can combine to make sentences.	★			★
Joining words and joining clauses using 'and'.		★	★	★
Sentence – Year 2				
Subordination (using when, if, that, because).			★	
Co-ordination (using or, and, but).		★		
Different sentences. Statement, question, exclamation, command.	★	★	★	★
Text – Year 1				
Sequencing sentences to form short narrative.	★			★
Text – Year 2				
Use of present and past tense in writing.	★	★	★	★
Punctuation – Year 1				
Capital letters, full stops, question marks, exclamation marks to demarcate sentences.	★			★
Punctuation – Year 2				
Capital letters, full stops, question marks, exclamation marks to demarcate sentences.	★	★	★	★

Sentence springboards

Word walls

Create eye catching word walls. One flash card equals one brick. Have several bricks to create the word wall with the children. Have blank cards so that the children can write new words and add to or make a new word wall shape. Use a word wall for the children to create simple sentences. Create challenges by mixing up words in sentences and asking the children to put them into the right order.

The word ladder

A similar game to 'Consequences'.

In groups of four the children are given strips of paper with four sections (see Word ladder Template – Teacher resources). The children write a short sentence on the first section, fold over the paper to hide it and pass it to the next child. They then write another short sentence in the next and so on. After the strip has been completed it is opened up and the children read out the four written sentences.

The game can be used in a variety of ways:

• Simple sentences: use the simple sentences to create a fun, nonsense story or poem.

• Compound sentences: ask the children to use 'but' between each sentence or they could also choose 'so' 'or'.

• Time connectives: the children choose a character and then use time connectives orally to recount what the character did. *First she went to the moon, then she swam with mermaids.*

Short sentences

Give a group or pair of children a five or six letter word, such as robot. Ask the children to write the letters going down the page. They then have to make up a simple sentence messages using the letters as the first words of each sentence: *Red apples are very tasty. Owls come out at night. Bob loves to eat pizza. Oranges make great drinks. The balloon flew away.* Explain that this way of playing with words is called an acrostic.

Instruction book

Have a 'How to do it' book made by the class. They all contribute how to make or cook something. Set out a frame that they could all use and highlight the use of time connectives. Encourage the children to draw diagrams to go with their instructions.

Find the letters

Ask the children to follow the clues which use prepositions to find letters that create a word. Let the children make up their own treasure hunts or hunt the letters with clues using prepositions.

Other activities

• Explore tongue twisters and fun poetry and rhymes.

• I-spy using prepositions.

• Fun t-shirt or captions for a bag or badge.

• Create short sentences for posters.

• Flip book sentences use card and rings. Add several word cards on each ring. Have words with capital letters on the first ring and words with full stops on the last ring. Children can have fun flipping over the words to make sentences.

• Look at a local map or map of the school and place pin or sticker on one place. Ask the children to use prepositions to show directions to the place.

• Kim's game. Look at a picture before it is taken away and then use prepositions to explain where objects or people are

• Cut out sentences in a weekly comic. Ask children to match them to the pictures in right order.

• The good and bad news game. The children use conjunctions to say a piece of good news followed by a funny piece of bad news about story characters. *The good news is that Big Billy Goat Gruff has got rid of the troll but the bad news is all the grass has been eaten by the other goats.*

Simple sentences

Learning objectives

- To understand that a sentence is a group of words that must make sense.

- To use capital letters and full stops in a sentence.

- To assemble written simple sentences, about a subject, together.

- To write simple sentences independently.

Resources

- **Lesson** – 'A Celtic hut'. 'Homes from the past' (Lesson resources CD-ROM) or use photos/pictures from history books or web sources.

- **Group 1 (Year 1)** – Copies of activity sheet 1 'Victorian toys' for each child.

- **Group 2 (Year 1/2)** – Copies of activity sheet 2 'Toys from the past' for each child.

- **Group 3 (Year 2)** – Copies of activity sheet 3 'A Victorian toy' for each child.

Lesson/activity notes

- **Lesson** – You could change the subject of the lesson to one which is relevant to a current class topic, such as toys from the past, plants, pets.

- **Group 1 (Year 1)** – Children work as a group and individually with adult support.

- **Group 2 (Year 1/2)** – Children work individually with adult/teacher discussion.

- **Group 3 (Year 2)** – Children work individually.

Lesson

Introduction

Show the picture 'A Celtic hut' to the children and explain that it was a home people lived in many years ago in Britain during Roman times. With the children read out the labels. Highlight how the labels are only one or two words. Explain that you are going to use one of the labels to write a simple sentence about the Celtic hut: *The hut has mud walls*. Highlight that a sentence is a group of words that makes sense. Use different highlighters to underline the different features of the sentence: capital letter to start, the main subject and a full stop.

Main lesson

Explain that you would like to create an information display of homes through the ages and need simple sentences to go with each home. Display one house picture at a time to the children.

Ask the children to think of one simple sentence about the house. Write the sentences on the board, with open ended prompts about using capital letters and full stops. Once all the sentences are written on the board, read through them with the class. Highlight the beginning and end of each sentence and the punctuation. Do the same with the other houses. At a later point create the display with the children's simple sentences.

Explain to the children that they are going to work on activities on simple sentences.

Put the children into their levelled groups and give out the activities. Spend time moving between the groups to discuss individual children's work and assess their level of understanding.

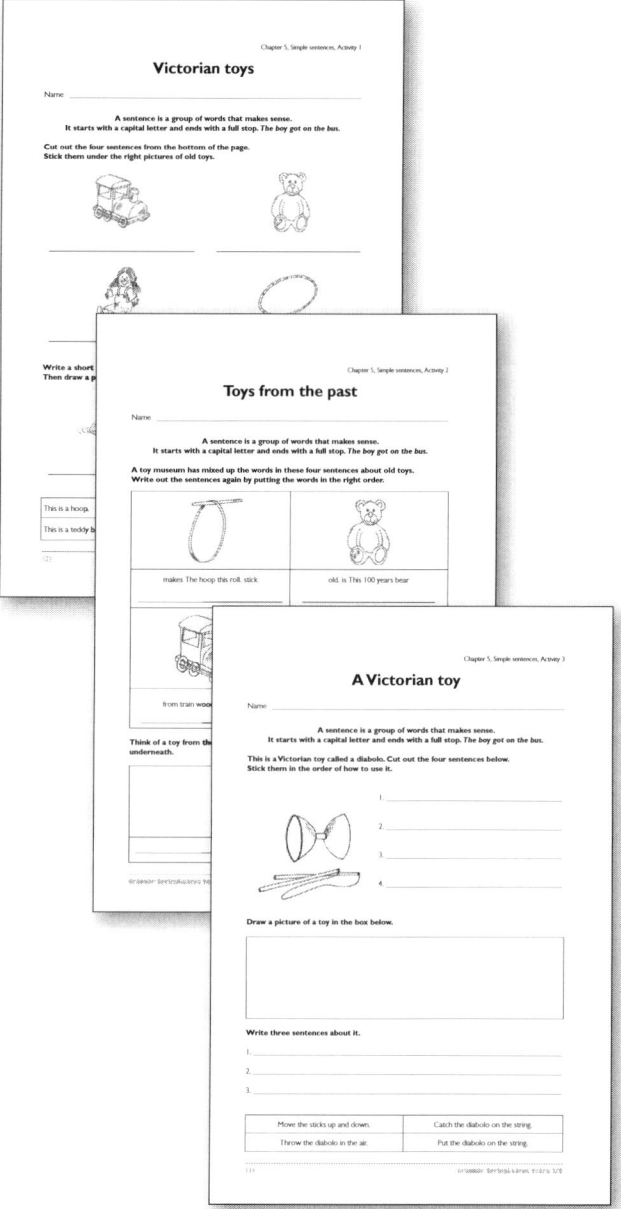

Activities

Group 1 (Year 1)

• Give out copies of 'Victorian toys' to each child.

• As a group, look at the first four pictures of Victorian toys and read the sentences at the bottom of the page.

• The children cut out the sentences and stick them under the matching toy.

• Ask the children to underline the capital letter and full stop in each sentence.

• Let them write a simple sentence in the same sentence pattern and draw a picture to go with it.

Group 2 (Year 1/2)

• Give out copies of 'Toys from the past' to each child.

• The children must rewrite the mixed up words of four sentences about old toys.

• Ask which two rules for writing sentences give clues to the first and last words in the sentences – capital letter and full stop.

• The children then draw a picture of an old toy with a simple sentence underneath it.

• At the end of the activity discuss how simple sentences in museum displays are called captions.

Group 3 (Year 2)

• Give out copies of 'A Victorian toy' to each child.

• Working individually, the children look at a picture of a Victorian diabolo.

• The children cut out the sentences then reassemble and stick them into a coherent group of sentences about how a diabolo was used.

• Discuss how the order of the sentences must make sense.

• The children then draw a picture of a Victorian toy of their own choice followed by three sentences about it.

Plenary

Before the end of the lesson, bring the groups together. Ask the children to give examples of their simple sentences about a Victorian toy. Write the sentences on the board. Ask the children what they need to remember when writing a sentence. Highlight the features as they are given, *capital letter, full stop*.

Support

For children who need more support, create simple sentence chains with a word per chain: *The man had a car*. The more words there are, the more sentences they could create. Design ideas could include a sentence train with carriages.

Extension

Encourage the children to create a fact file on a non–fiction subject using simple sentences for each fact. Discuss the order in which the information and sentences can be placed.

Victorian toys

Name _____

A sentence is a group of words that makes sense.
It starts with a capital letter and ends with a full stop. *The boy got on the bus.*

Cut out the four sentences from the bottom of the page.
Stick them under the right pictures of old toys.

_____   _____

_____   _____

Write a short sentence for the picture below.
Then draw a picture for the last toy.

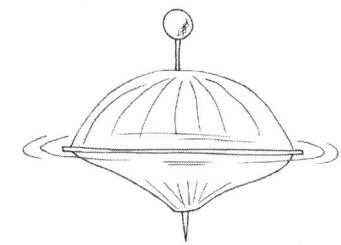

_____   This is a rocking horse.

This is a hoop.	This is a doll.
This is a teddy bear.	This is a train.

Grammar Springboards Years 1/2

Toys from the past

Name _____

**A sentence is a group of words that makes sense.
It starts with a capital letter and ends with a full stop.** *The boy got on the bus.*

**A toy museum has mixed up the words in these four sentences about old toys.
Write out the sentences again by putting the words in the right order.**

makes The hoop this roll. stick

_____

old. is This 100 years bear

_____

from train wood. This is made

_____

swung ball The into cup. wooden is the

_____

Think of a toy from the past. Draw its picture and write a simple sentence about it underneath.

_____

A Victorian toy

Name _____

**A sentence is a group of words that makes sense.
It starts with a capital letter and ends with a full stop. *The boy got on the bus.***

**This is a Victorian toy called a diabolo. Cut out the four sentences below.
Stick them in the order of how to use it.**

1. _____

2. _____

3. _____

4. _____

Draw a picture of a toy in the box below.

Write three sentences about it.

1. _____

2. _____

3. _____

Move the sticks up and down.	Catch the diabolo on the string.
Throw the diabolo in the air.	Put the diabolo on the string.

Co-ordination in sentences

Learning objectives
- To understand that two simple sentences joined into a long sentence is called a compound sentence.

- To understand that joining words (conjunctions) such as 'and', 'but', 'so' and 'or' can create compound sentences.

- To recognise the effect in a text by using compound sentences.

Resources
- **Lesson** – 'The sticky lollipop', 'Sticky lollipop short sentences', 'Joining words flash cards' (Lesson resources CD-ROM).

- **Group 1 (Year 1)** – One copy of activity sheet 1 'Joining two sentences' for the group. Whiteboard or computer. Mini books (see notes below), colouring pencils.

- **Group 2 (Year 1/2)** – A copy of activity sheet 2 'Joining two equal sentences' for each child. Mini books (see notes below), colouring pencils.

- **Group 3 (Year 2)** – A copy of activity sheet 3 'Co-ordination sentences ' for each child. Mini books (see notes below), colouring pencils.

Lesson/activity notes
- **Lesson** – In this lesson we have used 'Joining words' instead of the term 'conjunctions.' Choose which term is suitable for the skills and understanding of the children.

- **Mini Books** – 'Zig zag book instructions' and 'Slit book instructions' (Teacher resources CD-ROM). The Zig zag or Slit mini books can be made in advance depending on timing of lesson and skills of children. Use A3 card or paper if possible. Children could use the computer to write and then print out their sentences for their books.

- **Group 1 (Year 1)** – Children work as a discussion group with teacher/adult support as scribe. Cut out the sentences and joining words from the activity sheet before the lesson. Be near a whiteboard or a computer for writing out compound sentences. The children work individually on their mini-books.

- **Group 1 (Year 1/2)** – Children work in pairs on their activity sheets. They work individually on writing their mini books and then share their work. Teacher discussion needed when activity sheet is completed.

- **Group 3 (Year 2)** – Children work individually on the activity sheet and their compound story book. They pair-share their books at the end of the activity.

Lesson

Introduction
Read the story 'The sticky lollipop' to the children. Show or copy 'Sticky lollipop short sentences' onto a whiteboard. Highlight that we can make one long sentence by joining two of the short sentences together. Explain that these long sentences are called compound sentences. Introduce and display the three 'Joining words flash cards' 'and', 'but' and 'or'. Explain that these words are used to join two short sentences into one compound sentence.

Main lesson
Suggest to the children that they help you join the 'Sticky lollipop short sentences' into compound sentences by using the joining words 'and', 'but' and 'or'. Model the first two short sentences by adding 'and'. Note how the full stop of the first sentence and the beginning capital letter are not used. Discuss the improved effect of the sentence. With the children, change the rest of the sentences. Encourage children to come up and put the joining word card between the sentences. Read through the resulting compound sentences and highlight how compound sentences can make their writing flow and be more interesting.

Explain to the children that they are going to do activities on compound sentences. Put the children into their levelled groups and give out the activities. Spend time moving between the groups to discuss individual children's work and assess their level of understanding.

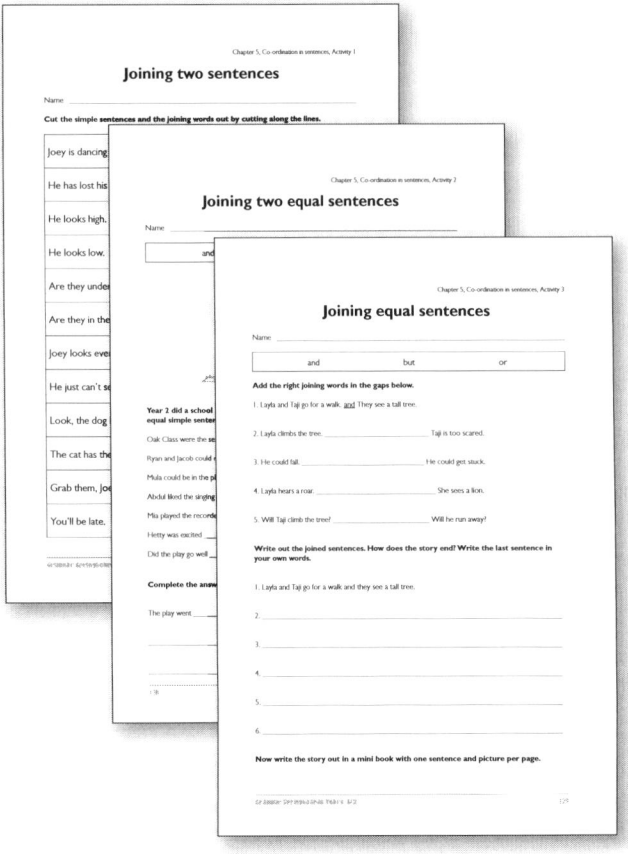

Activities

Group 1 (Year 1)

- Lay out the joining words in front of the children and read them out.

- Show the first two short sentences and with the children read them out.

- Ask the children in turn what joining word could be used to turn the sentences into one compound sentence. Write out the correct sentence on the white board or the computer.

- Highlight the omission of the first sentence's full stop and the second sentence's capital letter.

- Do the same procedure with the five other pairs of sentences.

- With the children read out the compound sentences and discuss their effect.

- Give out the mini books and let the children individually either copy the sentences or stick in printed sentences on each page and illustrate the story.

Group 2 (Year 1/2)

- Give out the activity sheet, 'Joining two equal sentences' to each child.

- Working individually, the children add the correct joining conjunctive to complete the sentences about a school play.

- Encourage them to read out the sentences to a partner or in a group. Do they make sense? Highlight how the first part and last part of the sentence have information that is of equal importance.

- The children are then asked to complete a sentence about the play using a 'but' conjunctive.

- Give them a mini book to rewrite the story with a compound sentence and picture per page. Let them share their completed books with the group.

Group 3 (Year 2)

- Give out the activity sheet 'Joining equal sentences' to each child.

- Working individually, the children add the correct joining word to turn five pairs of simple sentences of a short story into five compound sentences.

- They then write out the compound sentences correctly.

- The children are then asked to finish the story with a compound sentence of their own.

- Once they have finished ask a few questions, e.g. *How did you form the compound sentences? Why did you choose that joining word? How much more effective is the story?*

Plenary

Before the end of the lesson, bring all the groups together. Ask *'What is a compound sentence? How do we make compound sentences? Give me some examples of a linking word.'*

Support

Write out simple sentences from a well known story and with the children work on joining the sentences up to create compound sentences. Make word wall displays (see word wall ideas).

Extension

Encourage the children to create compound sentence poems using joining words such as 'but' or 'so'. Highlight how the first word of a second simple sentence can also be omitted to create more of a flow.

Joining two sentences

Name _____

Cut the simple sentences and the joining words out by cutting along the lines.

Joey is dancing in a show.
He has lost his shoes.
He looks high.
He looks low.
Are they under the bed?
Are they in the bin?
Joey looks everywhere.
He just can't see them.
Look, the dog has one shoe.
The cat has the other.
Grab them, Joey.
You'll be late.

and
or
but

Joining two equal sentences

Name _____

and	but	or

Year 2 did a school play about castles. Use the joining words above to join up the two equal simple sentences into one sentence.

Oak Class were the servants _____ Pine Class were the lords and ladies.

Ryan and Jacob could make the props _____ they could paint the scenery.

Mula could be in the play _____ he could help with the lights.

Abdul liked the singing _____ he did not like the dancing.

Mia played the recorder _____ Ethan played the drum.

Hetty was excited _____ she was nervous.

Did the play go well _____ did the play not go badly?

Complete the answer in your own words.

The play went _____ but _____

_____

_____

Joining equal sentences

Name _____

and	but	or

Add the right joining words in the gaps below.

1. Layla and Taji go for a walk. <u>and</u> They see a tall tree.

2. Layla climbs the tree. _____ Taji is too scared.

3. He could fall. _____ He could get stuck.

4. Layla hears a roar. _____ She sees a lion.

5. Will Taji climb the tree? _____ Will he run away?

Write out the joined sentences. How does the story end? Write the last sentence in your own words.

1. Layla and Taji go for a walk and they see a tall tree.

2. _____

3. _____

4. _____

5. _____

6. _____

Now write the story out in a mini book with one sentence and picture per page.

Subordination in sentences

Learning objectives

- To identify a main subject in a sentence.

- To identify a subordinate clause such as an extra piece of information.

- To understand that the main clause can be joined to the minor clause with joining words.

- To use subordinate joining words – when, if, that, because.

Resources

- **Lesson** – Board or paper for writing.

- **Group 1 (Year 1)** – Sentence clauses and joining words cut out from activity sheet 1, 'Making simple subordination sentences' for the activity. Children can have their own cards or use one set per group or for a pair of children. Paper.

- **Group 2 (Year 1/2)** – Copies of activity sheet 2, 'Joining main sentences with extra information' for each child. Red and blue pencils.

- **Group 3 (Year 2)** – Copies of activity sheet 3, 'Making subordination sentences' for each child. Red and blue pencils.

Lesson/activity notes

- **Lesson** – A discussion group and in pairs.

- **Group 1 (Year 1)** – Children work individually or pairs or in small groups with adult support.

- **Group 1 (Year 1/2)** – Children work individually or as a pair.

- **Group 3 (Year 2)** – Children work individually and pair-share their work.

Lesson

Introduction

Write the joining words – when, if, that, because – for the children to see. Read them out and explain that they can be used to join a sentence with an extra piece of information. Write a sentence such as 'I am going swimming.' and read it out. Now write after it with a gap in between, 'I have done the washing up.'. Read it out and explain that this is the extra information. Ask the children which joining word would be best to join the main sentence and information. Follow their suggestions.

Main lesson

Ask the children in pairs to come up with a main sentence and an extra piece of information. After a few minutes ask each pair for their sentences and then write them on the board. Ask the children as a group which joining word could be used to join up the sentences.

Once the sentences have been written out, go through them with the children and highlight the main sentences and the extra pieces of information.

Explain to the children that they are going to work with the sentences and joining words using activity sheets.

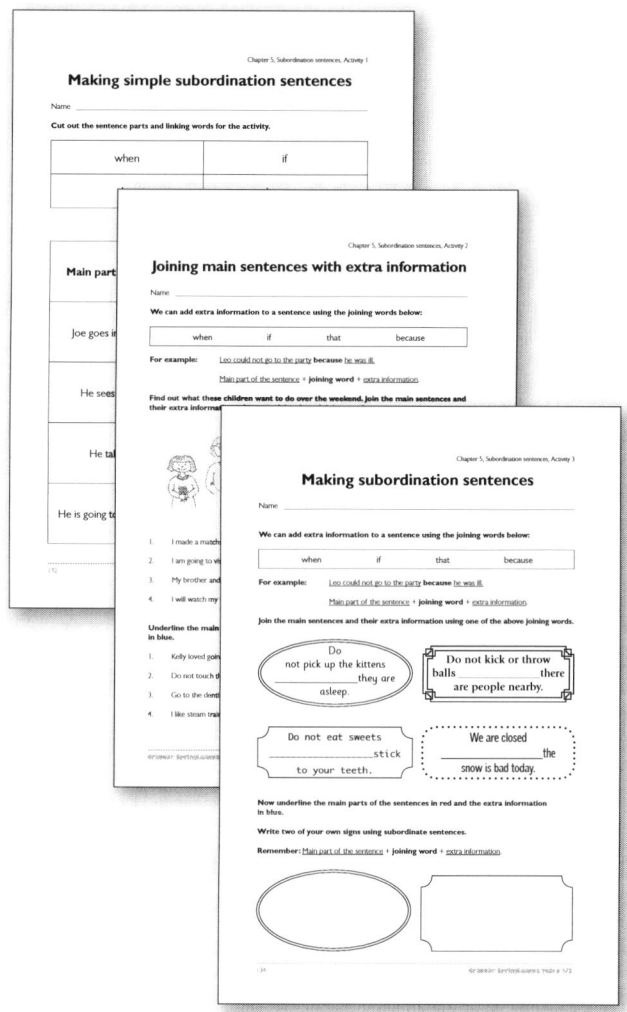

Activities

Group 1 (Year 1)

- Cut out the sentence parts and joining words on the sheet and put them in their shuffled piles in front of the children.

- Ask the children to lay out the four 'Main part of a sentence' cards on the table. Ask them to read through the sentences and put them in time order first.

- Note that the sentences do not end with a full stop because they are going to add extra information to them.

- The children lay out the extra information cards and match them in order to the main sentence.

- The children then use the joining words to join up the two clauses. Let them experiment and try out the linking words. Encourage them to read the final sentence to hear if it makes sense.

- Let the children draw a comic strip of the four sentences and write out the complete sentences under each picture.

Group 2 (Year 1/2)

- Give out the copies of 'Joining main sentences with extra information' for each child and let them read the information and example at the top of the sheet.

- Working individually or with a partner, the children choose the correct subordination joining words to join main clauses to extra information.

- They then use a red pencil to underline the main clauses in a sentence and a blue pencil to underline the extra bits of information.

- When they have completed the activity, encourage the children to write their own main clause about what they want to do over the weekend using a subordinate joining word to join up extra information about it.

Group 3 (Year 2)

- Give out the copies of 'Making subordination sentences' to each child and let them read the information and example at the top of the sheet.

- Working individually, the children choose a joining word to join main and subordinate clauses used on signs. They then use red and blue pencils to show which parts of the sentences are main clauses and extra bits of information.

- Finally they write two of their own signs using subordinate sentences.

Plenary

Ten minutes before the end of the lesson, bring the children together and let them share their work and sentences.

Support

Let children orally choose extra information for a set of given main sentences and discuss which joining word would be the best to use to join them into one sentence.

Extension

Let the children go through books to find examples of subordination in sentences and to try and use subordination in their own writing.

Making simple subordination sentences

Name _____

Cut out the sentence parts and linking words for the activity.

when	if
that	because

Main part of a sentence	Extra part of the sentence
Joe goes into the kitchen	he eats all of it.
He sees an apple pie	he is hungry.
He takes the pie	on the table.
He is going to get tummy ache	no one is looking.

Joining main sentences with extra information

Name _____

We can add extra information to a sentence using the joining words below:

when	if	that	because

For example: Leo could not go to the party **because** he was ill.

Main part of the sentence + **joining word** + extra information.

Find out what these children want to do over the weekend. Join the main sentences and their extra information using one of the above joining words.

1.   I made a matchstick model boat _____ I like boats.

2.   I am going to visit my Gran _____ she is feeling better.

3.   My brother and I are going to the swimming pool _____ has just been opened.

4.   I will watch my favourite DVD_____ I stay with my Aunty.

Underline the main parts of these sentences in red and the extra bits of information in blue.

1.   Kelly loved going to the local café because it was so cosy and friendly.

2.   Do not touch the iron when it is hot.

3.   Go to the dentist if you have a sore tooth.

4.   I like steam trains that make lots of smoke.

Making subordination sentences

Name _____

We can add extra information to a sentence using the joining words below:

when	if	that	because

For example: Leo could not go to the party **because** he was ill.

Main part of the sentence + **joining word** + extra information.

Join the main sentences and their extra information using one of the above joining words.

Do
not pick up the kittens
_____they are
asleep.

Do not kick or throw
balls _____there
are people nearby.

Do not eat sweets
_____stick
to your teeth.

We are closed
_____the
snow is bad today.

Now underline the main parts of the sentences in red and the extra information in blue.

Write two of your own signs using subordinate sentences.

Remember: Main part of the sentence + **joining word** + extra information.

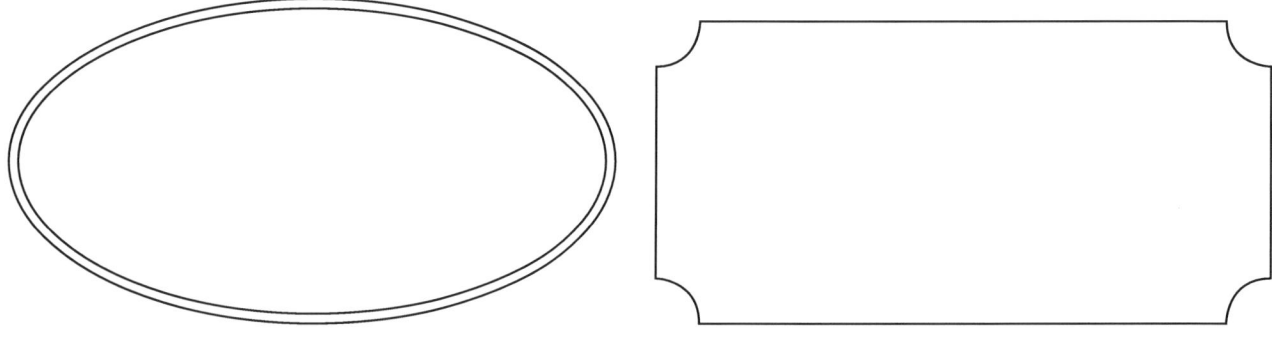

Simple time connectives

Learning objectives

- To understand that time words help tell when something is happening in stories and recounts.

- To identify and use time connectives to sequence and connect main parts of a story.

- To write a narrative using time connectives.

Resources

- **Lesson** – 'Chicken Licken text', 'Chicken Licken pictures'; Time connectives flash cards – (Lesson resources CD-ROM).

- **Group 1 (Year 1)** – Copies of activity sheet 1.1 'Space story' and 1.2, 'Space story pictures and sentences' for each child. Scissors, glue.

- **Group 2 (Year 1/2)** – Copies of activity sheet 2 'My big day' for each child. Colouring pencils.

- **Group 3 (Year 2)** – Copies of activity sheet 3 'A day in the life of ...' for each child.

Lesson/activity notes

- **Lesson** – In this lesson we have used 'Time words' instead of the term 'Time connectives'. Choose which term is suitable for the skills and understanding of the children. Copy the 'Chicken Licken pictures' before the lesson. After the lesson, the 'Chicken Licken' sentences could be copied or printed out and the pictures coloured in to create a display.

- **Group 1 (Year 1)** – Initial group discussion with teacher/adult. The children then work in pairs on the activity.

- **Group 2 (Year 1/2)** – The children initially work as a discussion group with teacher support. They work individually on their pictures and may need support in writing sentences.

- **Group 3 (Year 2)** – Initial group discussion with teacher/adult. The children then work in pairs on the activity.

Lesson

Introduction

Display the 'Time connectives flash cards' for all the children to see. Explain that these words tell when something is happening in stories or everyday life. Choose a simple example of how the time words could be used: getting up and going to school routine, making a sandwich. Write the time sequence sentences out. As you write the sentences, ask the children which time connective could be used to show the right time sequence. Read through the whole sequence.

Main lesson

Explain how time words can also be used to show the order of events in stories. Ask the children to think about the order of events to the traditional tale 'Chicken Licken' as you read it to them. Once you have read the story, show the 'Chicken Licken' pictures in a mixed up order. Ask the children to put them in the right sequence of events. Point to the time word flash cards and ask the children to recount the story using the time words e.g. *first, then, next, later, finally, afterwards*. Write their sentences under each picture and re–read the story.

Explain to the children that they are going to work on activities that use time connectives. Put the children into their levelled groups and give out the activities. Spend time moving between the groups to discuss individual children's work and assess their level of understanding.

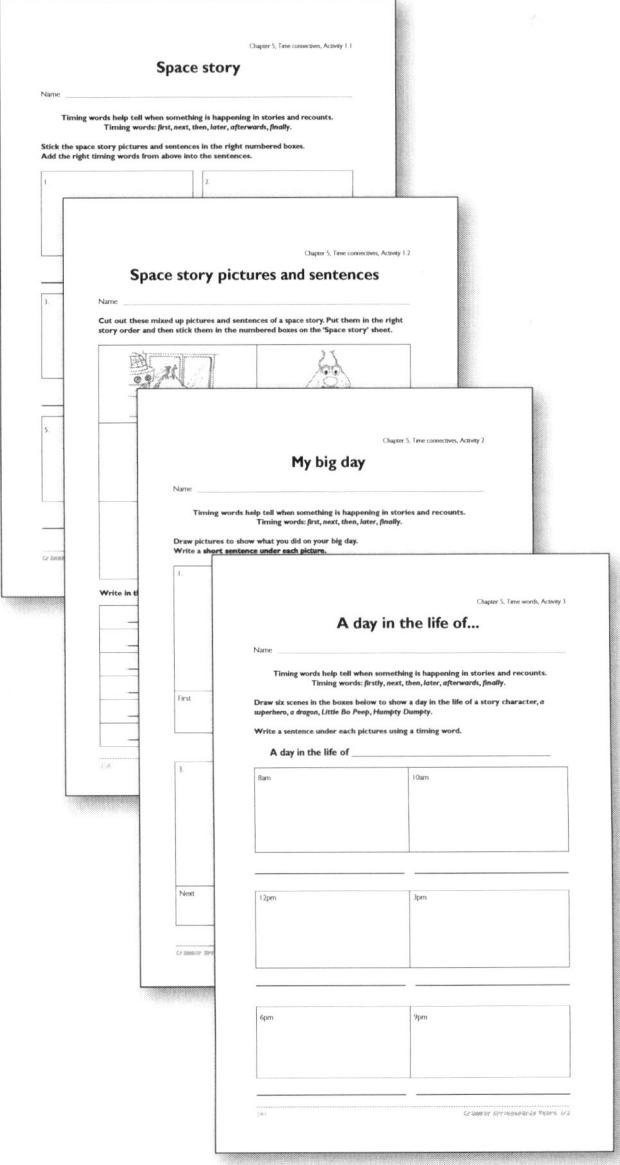

Activities

Group 1 (Year 1)

- Give out the activity sheets 'Space story' and 'Space story pictures and sentences' to each child.

- With the children read through the definition and the timing word examples on 'Space story 'sheet.

- Highlight that many stories go in time order and discuss examples, such as Cinderella.

- Working in pairs, ask the children to cut up the pictures and sentences from 'Space story pictures and sentences' and put them in the right time order.

- Encourage them to read through the story before they stick them on the 'Space story sheet' to see if it makes sense.

- After they have stuck the pictures and sentences down, the children write in the missing timing words in each sentence.

- If time, the children can make up and tell another space story using the timing words and share it with the group.

Group 2 (Year 1/2)

- Give out the activity sheet 1, 'My big day' to each child.

- Working as a group, look at the activity sheet and read out the activity.

- Ask the children to think of a special day and encourage each child to discuss the events in chronological order using the timing words, 'first', 'then', 'next' and 'finally'.

- Working individually the children then draw their day in the right boxes.

- Act as a scribe or encourage the children to write simple sentences under each picture.

- If time, let the children read out and show their work to the group.

Group 3 (Year 2)

- Give out the activity sheet, 'A day in the life of ...' to each child and put them into pairs.

- As a group, read the definition and the timing word examples with the children.

- Highlight the times in the each picture box and briefly discuss a day of a character as an example.

- Working in pairs, the children decide on their character and draw pictures of its day on their activity sheets.

- They then write sentences under each picture using the timing words from a list.

- Once they have finished, encourage the children to share their work with other children in their group.

Plenary

Before the end of the lesson, bring all the groups together. Ask some of the children to read and share their work with the class. Write the timing words on a board as the children read out their sentences. Discuss how they help the reader and writer know when an event is happening.

Support

Look at other simple stories with a clear sequence of events. Encourage the children to draw pictures to show the sequence and write the timing words under each one. Display and discuss the story.

Extension

Highlight how time words can also be used in instructions on doing something. Let the children draw and write simple instructions using time words for making a wacky sandwich or amazing snack.

Space story

Name _____

**Timing words help tell when something is happening in stories and recounts.
Timing words: *first, next, then, later, afterwards, finally*.**

**Stick the space story pictures and sentences in the right numbered boxes.
Add the right timing words from above into the sentences.**

1.

2.

3.

4.

5.

6.

Space story pictures and sentences

Name _____

Cut out these mixed up pictures and sentences of a space story. Put them in the right story order and then stick them in the numbered boxes on the 'Space story' sheet.

Write in the timing words: *first, next, then, later, afterwards, finally.*

_____ the alien ate all the apples.

_____ a UFO landed by a shop.

_____ the UFO took off.

_____ the alien put apples in the bag.

_____ an apple tree grew on its head.

_____ an alien jumped out with a big bag.

My big day

Name _____

Timing words help tell when something is happening in stories and recounts.
Timing words: *first, next, then, later, finally*.

Draw pictures to show what you did on your big day.
Write a short sentence under each picture.

1.	2.
First	Then

3.	4.
Next	Finally

A day in the life of...

Name _____

**Timing words help tell when something is happening in stories and recounts.
Timing words: *firstly, next, then, later, afterwards, finally.***

Draw six scenes in the boxes below to show a day in the life of a story character, *a superhero, a dragon, Little Bo Peep, Humpty Dumpty.*

Write a sentence under each pictures using a timing word.

A day in the life of _____

8am	10am

_____   _____

12pm	3pm

_____   _____

6pm	9pm

_____   _____

Chapter 6 – Punctuation

Punctuation information

Questions	Questions are sentences that ask something and expect an answer. All questions end with a question mark (?). There are several types of questions:		
	Interrogative questions, which are questions that mainly start with 'wh-' words: *when, where, who, what, why, how, which.* 'What' is used when questions are asked about things. 'Who' is used when questions are asked about people. 'When' is used when questions are asked about time. 'Where' is used when questions are asked about places. 'Why' is used when questions are asked to find a reason. 'Which' is used when questions are asked about a choice. 'How' is used when questions are asked to find out about things and people.		
	Tag questions are questions that start with a statement and have a question tagged onto the end.		*He is funny, isn't he?*
	A yes/no question is a question that can only have a yes or no answer.		*Are you happy? Yes.*
	An alternative question is a question which gives more than two answers within the question.		*Would you like water, juice, coffee or tea?*
Full stops (.)	Full stops are used at the end of sentences.		
Exclamation marks (!)	Exclamations are used to make a point, speaking with force or show surprise. They are usually used in a short sentence.		*Look out! I can't do it! That is amazing!*
Speech marks ("_")	Speech marks show speech within writing.		*"I wish I could go home," sighed Jake.*
Commas (,)	Commas can be used for different purposes:	To separate words in a list within a sentence. They take the place of the words 'and' and 'or' in a list of more than three words and phrases. The last word in the list has 'and' or 'or' before it.	*In my bag I have a pen, book, purse, phone, tissues and a lipstick.*

Punctuation information continued

Apostrophes (')	Apostrophes are used to mark: 1. Contractions. 2. Possession.		
	Apostrophes of contraction	This apostrophe marks where letters have been left out. This happens when the writer makes writing sound more natural by contracting (i.e. shortening) words. The apostrophe replaces the letters omitted.	*"I'm tired," grumbled Sam. "We've walked since 4 o'clock."*
	Apostrophes of possession	This apostrophe indicates ownership. The apostrophe refers to the owner. Its position varies according to the owner.	
		For a singular owner, add '-'s'.	*Sam's feet were aching.*
		For a plural owner ending in '-s', add an apostrophe.	*Both boys' bags were too heavy.*
		For a plural owner not ending in '-s', add '-'s'.	*Other children's bags were lighter.*
		Ask yourself, "Who is the owner?" Place the apostrophe immediately after the answer.	

Punctuation objective chart

Objectives and year group	Sentence Punctuation	Questions	Commas in a list (Year 2)	Apostrophes Contractions (Year 2)
Sentence – Year 1				
How words can combine to make sentences.	★	★		
Sentence – Year 2				
Different sentences. Statement, question, exclamation, command.	★	★	★	★
Text – Year 1				
Sequencing sentences to form short narrative.	★	★		
Text – Year 2				
Use of present and past tense in writing.	★	★	★	★
Punctuation – Year 1				
Capital letters, full stops, question marks, exclamation marks to demarcate sentences.	★	★		
Capital letters for names and for the personal pronoun 'I'.	★	★	★	
Punctuation – Year 2				
Capital letters, full stops, question marks, exclamation marks to demarcate sentences.	★	★	★	
Commas to separate items in a list.			★	
Apostrophes to mark where letters are missing.				★

Punctuation springboards

Word walls

Create eye catching word walls. One flash card equals one brick. Have several bricks to create the word wall with the children. Have blank cards that the children can write new words and add to or make a new word wall shape.

The walls can be used in a variety of ways:

- **Questions:** have a short question on a brick and an answer on each brick. Do several and encourage the children to match them up. Have a wall for the question words, *what, when, which, where, who, why, how.*

- **Commas:** have a wall of objects which the children can use to make up lists using commas.

- **Punctuation sign wall:** have punctuation signs on the wall as reference for the children and discussion points.

The word ladder

A similar game to 'Consequences'. In groups of four the children are given strips of paper with four sections (see Word ladder Template – Teacher resources). The children write a word or sentence on the first section, fold over the paper to hide it and pass it to the next child. They then write another word or sentence on the next and so on. After the strip has been completed it is opened up and the children read out the four written words or sentences.

- **Questions** – The game can be used for questions. The first section is a question followed by an answer then a question and then an answer. The children read out the fun results.

- **Commas** – The children write words to create a list. They write out their final lists adding commas.

- **Speech marks** – Speech sentences with speech marks can make a fun dialogue.

Write a speech

The children are given bits of paper. They write one or two pieces of dialogue on the paper with speech marks. The pieces of paper are all put in a box/hat. They are shuffled and as a group or class the lines are put into some form of sequence for a fun dialogue story which is read out loud.

Other activities

- Who am I? What am I? Where am I? Question games.

- Yes and no questions.

- Write pairs of cards, for example male and female names of animals, two parts of a compound noun. The children are given one card and they have to ask other children questions to find their matching pair.

- Joke and riddle books or displays.

- Play question rhyme games such as What's the time, Mr Wolf?

- Collect a list of class questions. Each child contributes a question to which they would like to find the answer. The questions are written out with the children.

- Make collections of things that could relate to a topic or specific children's interests such as stamp collecting, mini-beasts, marbles or trump cards. Encourage the children to write lists of the collections.

- Have a washing line with objects and words and get the children to create lists.

- Cut out speech bubbles from comics and get the children to rewrite the speech in their own words using speech marks.

- Fun lists and menus.

Sentence punctuation – capitals, full stops, exclamation marks

<table>
<tr><td>

Learning objectives
- To use capital letters and full stops to demarcate sentences.

- To recognise an exclamation mark.

- To recognise an exclamation and to add an exclamation mark to it.

Resources
- **Lesson** – Board or paper.

- **Group 1 (Year 1)** – Copies of activity sheet 1 'Capital letters, full stops and exclamation marks' for each child.

- **Group 2 (Year 1/2)** – Copies of activity sheet 2 'Adding capital letters, full stops and exclamation marks' for each child.

- **Group 3 (Year 2)** – Copies of activity sheet 3 'Using capital letters, full stops and exclamation marks' for each child.

Lesson/activity notes
- **Lesson** – As a discussion group.

- **Group 1 (Year 1)** – Children work individually or in pairs with adult support.

- **Group 2 (Year 1/2)** – Children work individually and pair-share their work.

- **Group 3 (Year 2)** – Children work individually and pair-share their work.

</td></tr>
</table>

Lesson

Introduction
Discuss with the children when we use a capital letter and a full stop in sentences. Ask why we need to use them. Mention how question marks are also used at the end of question sentences. Highlight that there is another punctuation sign which shows the end of a special type of sentence.

Main lesson
Draw a large exclamation mark on the board. Write and say at the same time 'Watch out'. Explain that this is an exclamation sentence which can be used to show moments such as surprise, warnings and danger. Add the exclamation mark to the words. Highlight how exclamation marks can

be used for single words or a couple of words to short sentence.

With the children come up with some exclamations and get them to add the exclamation mark. Highlight how it helps to say the words or sentences to hear the exclaiming. Explain to the children that they are going to do activities on punctuation in sentences such as capital letters, full stops and exclamation marks.

Activities

Group 1 (Year 1)
- Give out the copies of 'Capital letters, full stops and exclamation marks' for each child.

- Read out the information at the top of the page. Children need to add capital letters and full stops to three simple statement sentences.

- Once they have done this exercise, look at the section on exclamation sentences and marks. Encourage children to read out the exclamations before they add the exclamation marks so that they can hear the exclaiming tone.

- Once they have completed the activity, ask the children to work in pairs to think of exclamation sentences and say them out loud.

Group 2 (Year 1/2)

- Give out the copies of 'Adding capital letters, full stops and exclamation marks' to each child.

- Read out the information at the top of the page. Children need to add capital letters and full stops to three simple statement sentences. Before they start, note that there are proper nouns also in the sentences and briefly revise what they include such as country names and place names.

- They then read through a list of sentences which need to be ended either with an exclamation mark or a full stop.

- Let the children find a partner to read out the sentences one at a time to help them decide what a normal sentence is and what an exclamation is.

Group 3 (Year 2)

- Give out the copies of 'Using capital letters, full stops and exclamation marks' for each child.

- Read out the information at the top of the page. Children need to add capital letters and full stops to three simple statement sentences. Before they start, note that there are proper nouns also in the sentences and briefly revise what they include such as country names and place names.

- They then read the information about exclamation marks and exclamation sentences and add exclamation marks to two sentences as well as drawing pictures to show the exclamations.

- Finally, they write their own exclamation sentence. Let them pair-share their work.

Plenary

Ten minutes before the end of the lesson, bring the children together to share their work. Listen to their examples of exclamation sentences and check that they know that they need to end a sentence with a suitable punctuation mark and start a sentence with a capital letter.

Support

Read out a list of sentences that include quite a few exclamations and ask the children to listen and put their hands up when they think a sentence needs an exclamation mark.

Extension

Let the children create a set of exclamation speech bubbles for a fantasy space story that can be displayed in the class.

Capital letters, full stops and exclamation marks

Name _____

We write statements when we write about facts.
Add capital letters at the start of the sentences and full stops at the end.
Draw pictures to go with the statements.

A (A/a) ball is round	_____ (b/B) bicycles have two wheels
_____ (d/D) dolphins live in the sea	_____ S/s) snowmen are made from snow

Exclamation marks (!)

Add the exclamation marks to the sentences and match them to the pictures.

Watch out! A snake!

What a big cake

I'm stuck at home

The house is on fire

Adding capital letters, full stops and exclamation marks

Name _____

We use statements when we write about facts and what we think about things.

Rewrite the statements below, adding the missing capital letters and full stops.

i live in great britain

_____

chickens give us eggs

_____

the tallest mountain in the world is mount everest

_____

_____

Exclamation marks (!)

We put exclamation marks at the end of sentences to show surprise or danger.

Complete each sentence with either a full stop or an exclamation mark.

1. I went shopping yesterday

2. Look out

3. There is a large spider behind you

4. What an amazing cake

5. I am just going to read a book.

Using capital letters, full stops and exclamation marks

Name _____

Statements

We use statements when we write about facts and what we think about things.

Add the missing capital letters and full stops to these statements below.

1. the longest river in the world is the river nile

2. it is in africa

3. It starts in burundi and ends at the mediterranean sea in egypt

Write a statement sentence about an amazing fact.

_____

_____

Exclamation marks (!)

We put exclamation marks at the end of sentences to show surprise or danger, for example, *Keep away! Watch out for the bull!*

Add an exclamation to these sentences and draw a picture to match each one.

What a wonderful birthday cake	Look out That comet is going to crash

Make up one more exclamation sentence.

_____

Questions

Learning objectives

- To understand that a question sentence ends with a question mark.

- To understand that questions usually have an answer.

- To recognise that questions often start with *what*, *when*, *who*, *where*, *which*, *why*, *how*.

- To write simple questions and answers.

Resources

- **Lesson** – 'Question words flash cards', (Teacher resources CD-ROM), whiteboard.

- **Group 1 (Year 1)** – Copies of activity sheet 1 'A busy street' for each child or a picture/photo of a busy scene, for example a Brueghel or Lowry painting. 'Question words flash cards' (Teacher resources CD-ROM), a bag, whiteboard (small or large).

- **Group 2 (Year 1/2)** – Copies of activity sheet 2 'Tell me a joke' for each child. Joke books.

- **Group 3 (Year 2)** – Copies of activity sheet 3.1 'A quiz' and activity sheet 3.2 'My quiz' for each child, spare paper, books, and resources on fiction or non–fiction topics.

Lesson/activity notes

- **Lesson** – Copy and cut up the 'Question words flash cards' before the lesson.

- **Group 1 (Year 1)** – Children work as a group with teacher/adult support. Put the 'Question words flash cards' into the bag before the activity. Use the activity picture or a painting/picture of a busy scene.

- **Group 2 (Year 1/2)** – Children work individually on matching the jokes and then with a partner to create two jokes.

- **Group 3 (Year 2)** – Children work individually on activity sheet 3.1 'A quiz'. They work in pairs on activity sheet 3.2 'My quiz'.

Lesson

Introduction

Start the lesson by playing 'Twenty questions'. Explain that you are an object or a story character and the children have to ask up to twenty questions to guess what or who you are. At the end of the game, highlight that questions are sentences that ask something. Write one of the questions the children asked on the board. Highlight the use of a question mark instead of a full stop. Display the 'Question words flash cards' for all the children to see. Read through each word and explain that they often start a question.

Main Lesson

Choose a favourite book character such as Cinderella and ask the children to think of seven questions they would like to ask her using the seven question words. Write out examples of some of the children's suggestions, for example *Where do you go on holiday? What is your favourite sweet? Who is your best friend?* As you write the questions out, reinforce the use of the question mark at the end. Ask the children to work in small groups to think of simple answers for each question. After a few minutes, write down their answers. Highlight the repeated word pattern in the answers, *My favourite sweet is chocolate.*

Explain to the children that they are going to work on activities on questions. Put the children into their levelled groups and give out the activities. Spend time moving between the groups to discuss individual children's work and assess their level of understanding.

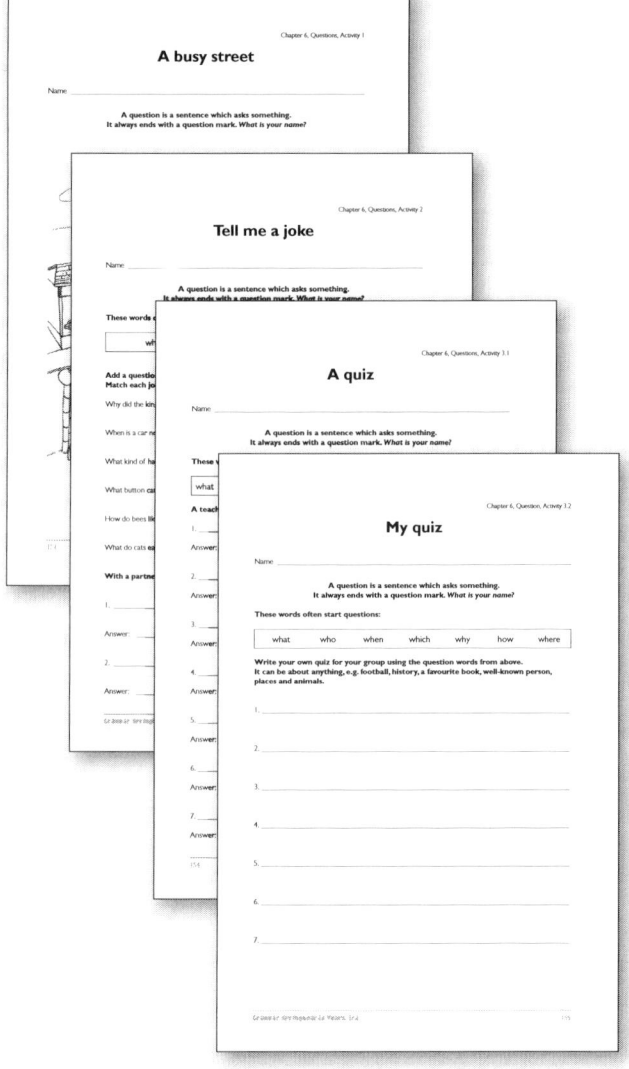

Activities

Group 1 (Year 1)

- Give out copies of activity sheet 1, 'A busy street' to each child.

- Put the 'Question words flash cards' in a bag in the middle of the table. Then ask a child to take a card and say it out loud.

- They then look at 'A busy street' and use it to ask a question beginning with their question word, *Where is the cat?*

- Write out the question on a whiteboard and ask 'What should a question end with?'

- Once the children have answered the question, the question card is put back in the bag and the next child repeats the procedure.

- When all the children have asked a question, read through the questions and highlight the question mark.

- Allow the children to colour in the picture, encouraging them to think of other questions they could ask.

Group 2 (Year 1/2)

- Give out the copies activity sheet 2, 'Tell me a joke' to each of the children.

- Highlight that jokes are questions with funny answers.

- Working individually, the children match the joke question to the right answer and then add the question marks.

- Finally they work with a partner to write two of their own jokes.

- Allow the children to share their jokes with the rest of the group.

- If time, challenge each pair to write a riddle question for another pair to solve.

Group 3 (Year 2)

- Give out copies of 'A quiz' and 'My quiz' to each child.

- Working individually, the children write the missing questions to written answers for a quiz on activity sheet 3.1 'A quiz'.

- They then work in pairs on activity sheet 3.2 'My quiz' to write seven questions for a quiz of their own choice, such as a favourite hobby or subject.

- Allow the children access to books and resources to help them put together their questions.

- Encourage them to write out their questions in rough before they add them to the sheet. Check if they have added a question mark.

- Allow the children to swop their quizzes with other pairs of children.

Plenary

Before the end of the lesson, bring all the groups together. Encourage the children to share the questions they used in their activities. Write a few more examples of questions on the board and reinforce the use of question marks and use of the question words. If time, have a quick class quiz or collect more jokes from the children.

Support

To reinforce the idea of questions, have a drama hot seat session where the children can ask a story character questions. Work as a scribe to help them record their questions. Let them add the question marks and underline the question words.

Extension

Encourage the children to use questions in their topic or class work. They could create a simple questionnaire or survey about improving the school environment or supporting the 3Rs, write a quiz for the class or design book review question sheets.

A busy street

Name _____

A question is a sentence which asks something.
It always ends with a question mark. *What is your name?*

Tell me a joke

Name _____

A question is a sentence which asks something.
It always ends with a question mark. *What is your name?*

These words often start questions:

what	who	when	which	why	how	where

Add a question mark to the eight joke questions.
Match each joke to their right answers.

Why did the king go to the dentist?   Wavy.

When is a car not a car?   Mice-crispies.

What kind of hair do seas have?   A belly button.

What button can't you buy in a shop?   To get his teeth crowned.

How do bees like to travel?   When it turns into a garage.

What do cats eat for breakfast?   By buzz.

With a partner, think of two jokes and write them below. Share them with friends.

1. _____

Answer: _____

2. _____

Answer: _____

A quiz

Name _____

**A question is a sentence which asks something.
It always ends with a question mark. *What is your name?***

These words often start questions:

what	who	when	which	why	how	where

A teacher has lost the questions to this quiz. Can you write them in?

1. _____

Answer: The opposite of big is small.

2. _____

Answer: Aladdin had a magic lamp.

3. _____

Answer: There are 7 days in a week.

4. _____

Answer: Worms live in the earth.

5. _____

Answer: The River Thames runs through London.

6. _____

Answer: Little Miss Muffet was scared of the spider.

7. _____

Answer: Guy Fawkes Night is on the 5th November.

My quiz

Name _____

A question is a sentence which asks something.
It always ends with a question mark. *What is your name?*

These words often start questions:

| what | who | when | which | why | how | where |

Write your own quiz for your group using the question words from above.
It can be about anything, e.g. football, history, a favourite book, well-known person,
places and animals.

1. _____

2. _____

3. _____

4. _____

5. _____

6. _____

7. _____

Commas in lists

Learning objectives

- To understand the use of commas replacing 'and' in sentences containing lists.

- To add commas accurately into sentences containing lists.

- To write sentences with commas in lists.

Resources

- **Lesson** – Whiteboard for all the children to see.

- **Group 1 (Year 1)** – Copy and cut activity sheets 1 'Object cards' and activity sheet 1.2 'Comma/and flash cards'. A box to put the cards in. A whiteboard or display board.

- **Group 2 (Year 1/2)** – Copies of activity sheet 2 'Nature trail lists' for each child.

- **Group 3 (Year 2)** – Copies of activity sheet 3 'The Story Book Ball' to each child.

Lesson/activity notes

- **Group 1 (Year 1)** – Children work as a discussion group with teacher/adult support.

- **Group 2 (Year 1/2)** – Children work individually on the activity and then in pairs create a nature list. Teacher discussion during the activity.

- **Group 3 (Year 2)** – Children work individually on the activity with teacher discussion at the beginning and the end. The children share their lists with the group.

Lesson

Introduction

Start the lesson playing 'When I went shopping I bought...' game with the children. Write *'When I went shopping I bought'* on the board and then write each item along the board with an 'and' between each item as each child contributes their idea, for example *'When I went shopping I bought a hat and a skirt and a bag of sweets and a...'* Put a limit of about ten items and then stop the game.

Main lesson

Read out the first sentence to the children, emphasising the word 'and'. Highlight that the sentence is a long shopping list. Highlight all the 'and' in the sentence. Discuss how they make the sentence sound long and awkward. Introduce and draw a comma on the board. Explain to the children that it can be used to replace the 'and's. Rub out each 'and' in the list and replace it with a comma. Stop at the last item

and emphasise that the very last item keeps the 'and'. Read out the list with commas with the children and discuss the improvement.

Explain to the children that they are going to work on activities on commas in lists.

Put the children into their levelled groups and give out the activities. Spend time moving between the groups to discuss individual children's work and assess their level of understanding.

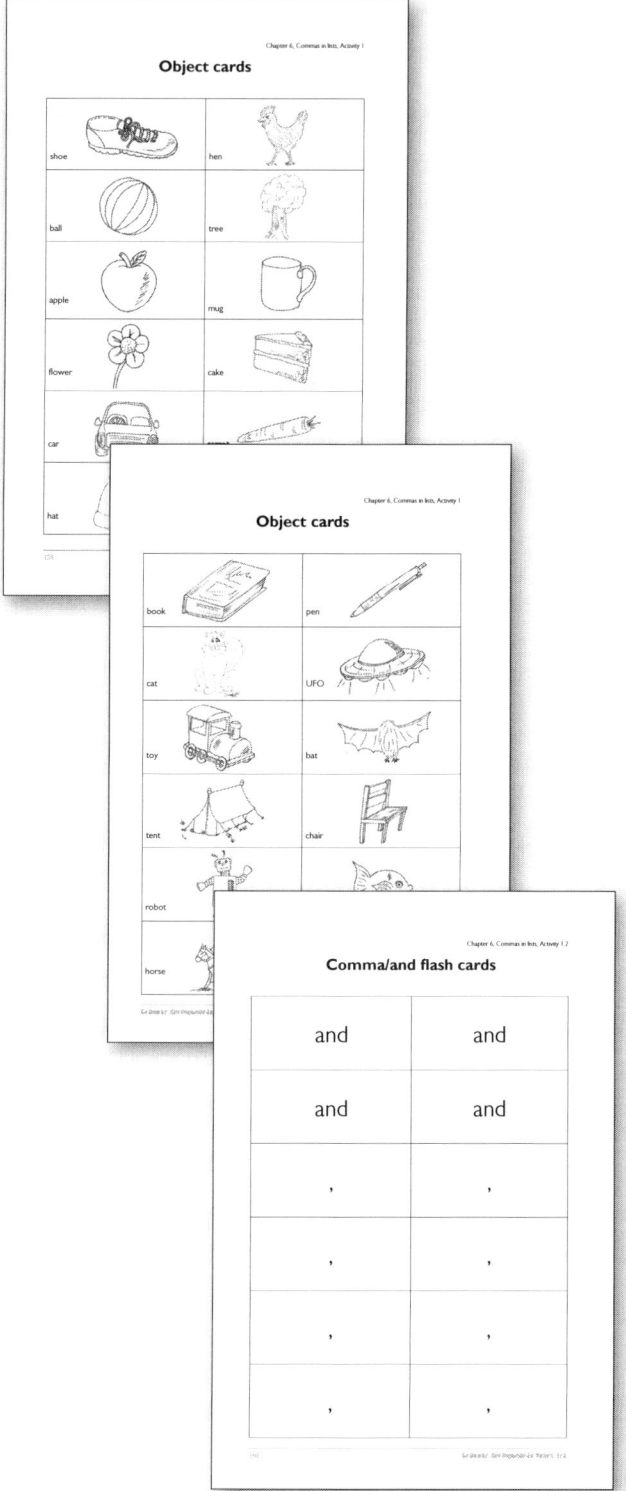

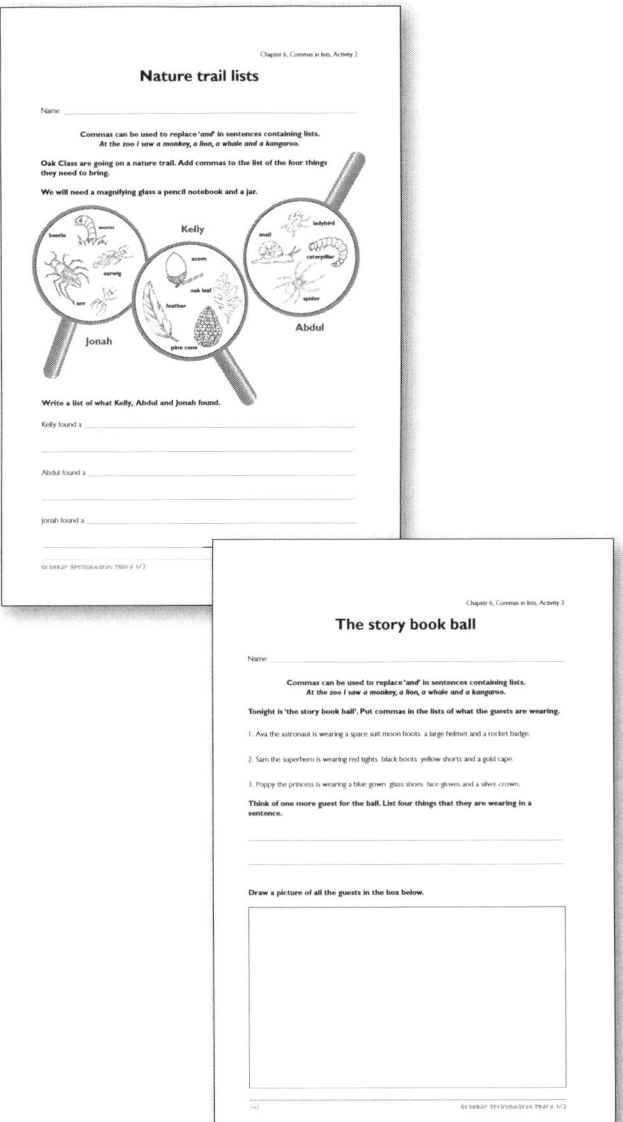

Activities

Group 1 (Year 1)

- Put a box with the set of 'Object cards' in the middle of the table. Have the pile of 'Comma/and flash cards' by the box.

- Explain to the children that working as a group they are going to make a list of the objects in the box using commas.

- Start the game by saying *'In the box there is a...'*

- A child takes a card out of the box, says what the object is, for example *'shoe'* and lays it on the table. They then put a comma card after it.

- The group then say *'In the box there is a shoe,'* and the next child adds to the list.

- When the last card comes out, reinforce that the 'and' card is used to end the list.

- Read out the list with the children and display the cards with commas or re-write on a board.

Group 2 (Year 1/2)

- Give out the copies of activity sheet 2 'Nature trail lists' to each child.

- Working individually, the children add commas to a list of items needed for a nature trail.

- They then write out three lists of what three children found in the nature trail.

- Once they have completed the activity ask the children why commas are used in lists instead of *'and'*.

- If time ask them to work in pairs to compile a list of other creatures, flowers or trees that they might see on a nature trail.

- Encourage them to share their lists with others in their group.

Group 3 (Year 2)

- Give out the copies of activity sheet 3, 'The Story Book Ball', to each child.

- Working individually, the children add commas to three sentences which list what three guests are wearing.

- Before they start, highlight that each item on the lists has an adjective describing it so the children need to think carefully where they put the commas.

- Once they have completed the activity, they create two more guests and list the five items that the guests are wearing. Encourage the use of adjectives in the lists.

- The children can then draw a picture of all the guests using the lists as information.

- Once they have finished, encourage the children to compare their last two lists.

Plenary

Before the end of the lesson, bring all the groups together. Encourage the children to share the lists they worked on in their activities. Write a couple on the whiteboard without commas and ask the children where the commas should go. Highlight the use of *'and'* to signal the end of the list. If time have one more oral game of *'When I went to...'* with the children.

Support

To help children understand the use of a comma in a list, work more with picture/words and the comma flash cards or bring in actual objects for different topics, such as ingredients for a sandwich, lists of animals in a zoo, objects in the art area.

Extension

Extending on from the worksheet, highlight that lists in sentences don't have to be just single words but one or two words, for instance describing a noun, *'a golden spade'* or a verb and noun, *'a jumping frog'*. Encourage the children to explore and create fun and unusual lists.

Object cards

shoe	hen
ball	tree
apple	mug
flower	cake
car	carrot
hat	ring

Object cards

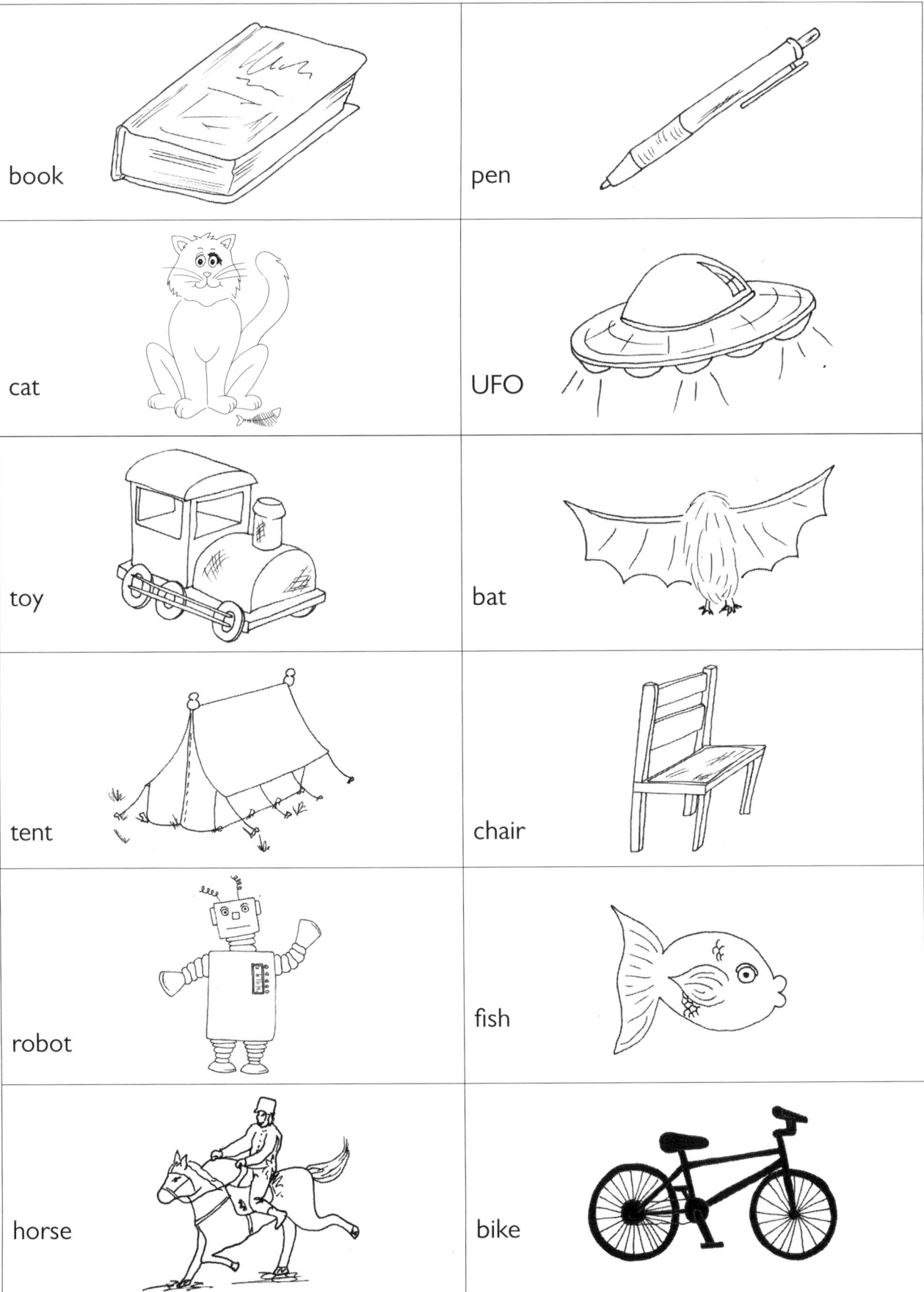

book		pen	
cat		UFO	
toy		bat	
tent		chair	
robot		fish	
horse		bike	

Comma/and flash cards

and	and
and	and
,	,
,	,
,	,
,	,

Nature trail lists

Name _____

Commas can be used to replace 'and' in sentences containing lists.
At the zoo I saw a monkey, a lion, a whale and a kangaroo.

Oak Class are going on a nature trail. Add commas to the list of the four things they need to bring.

We will need a magnifying glass a pencil notebook and a jar.

Write a list of what Kelly, Abdul and Jonah found.

Kelly found a _____

_____.

Abdul found a _____

_____.

Jonah found a _____

_____.

The story book ball

Name _____

Commas can be used to replace 'and' in sentences containing lists.
At the zoo I saw a monkey, a lion, a whale and a kangaroo.

Tonight is 'the story book ball'. Put commas in the lists of what the guests are wearing.

1. Ava the astronaut is wearing a space suit moon boots a large helmet and a rocket badge.

2. Sam the superhero is wearing red tights black boots yellow shorts and a gold cape.

3. Poppy the princess is wearing a blue gown glass shoes lace gloves and a silver crown.

Think of one more guest for the ball. List four things that they are wearing in a sentence.

_____

_____

Draw a picture of all the guests in the box below.

Apostrophes – contractions

Learning objectives
- To know what an apostrophe is.

- To understand how some words can be contracted by using the apostrophe.

- To match the full words with their contractions.

Resources
- **Lesson** – Display board or large paper (A3) to create a word wall. Cut up words from activity sheet 1 'Find the words and contractions'. Glue or pins.

- **Group 1 (Year 1)** – Copies of activity sheet 1 'Find the words and contractions' for each child. Coloured pencils.

- **Group 2 (Year 1/2)** – Copies of activity sheet 2 'Match the words and contractions' for each child.

- **Group 3 (Year 2)** – Copies of activity sheet 3 'Search the bag' for each child.

Lesson/activity notes
- **Lesson** – As a discussion group and in pairs.

- **Group 1 (Year 1)** – Children work in pairs or within a small group with adult support.

- **Group 2 (Year 1/2)** – Children work individually and pair-share work.

- **Group 3 (Year 2)** – Children work individually and pair-share work.

Lesson

Introduction
Draw a large apostrophe on the board so that all the children can see it. Introduce the name and explain that we can use it to show where there are missing letters in words. Write the following full words in a vertical list: '*I am*', '*it is*', '*he will*'. Read them out. Explain that we can shorten the words into one word by taking out some letters and replacing them with the apostrophe. Write each contraction for the words – '*I'm, it's, he'll*'. Highlight how we tend to say and write these shortened words when we are relaxed and at ease.

Main lesson
Give small groups or pairs of children cards showing full words or a contraction.

Using a board or a large piece of paper create a word wall by getting the children to match the contractions with their full words and using them as pair bricks.

Once the word wall of the pairs is created, look at each pair in turn and how the words are shortened.
Explain to the children that they are going to do activities on contractions.

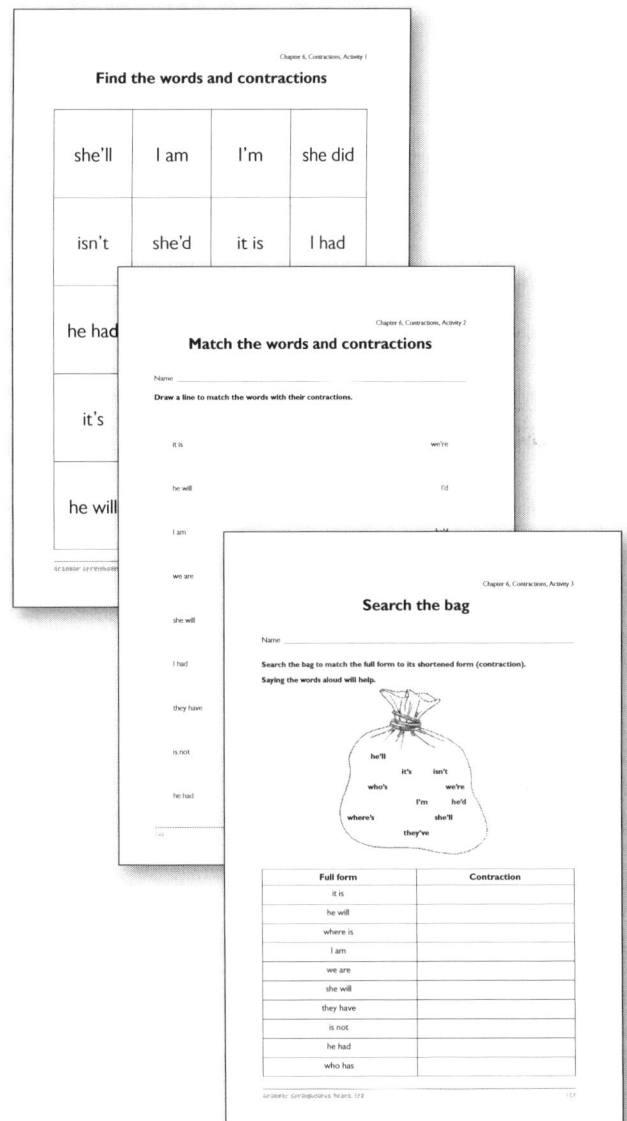

Activities

Group 1 (Year 1)
- Give out copies of 'Find the words and contractions' to each child. Remind the children of how some words can be shortened by cutting out certain letters and replacing them with an apostrophe.

- Point to the first word on the activity chart. Ask: 'Is *it a contraction or a full word?*' How do we know it is a contraction? (use of apostrophe). Ask children to say the word and what they think it is short for. Encourage them to look for the full word on the chart and use one colour to colour the two words.

- Do the same routine with all the words and their contractions, using a different colour for each pair.

Group 2 (Year 1/2)
- Give out the copies of 'Match the words and contractions' to each child.

- Working individually, the children draw lines to match the full words with their correct contractions.

- Encourage the children to say the contractions if they are unsure what they are short for.

- After the activity, ask the children to orally use one of the contractions in a sentence followed by another sentence using the matching full words.

Group 3 (Year 2)
- Give out the copies of 'Search the bag' to each child and explain what must be done.

- Encourage the children to read the contractions aloud to themselves as they search for the full words.

- At the end of the activity, let the children pair-share to check their answers with each other. Let the children orally use some of the full words and their contractions in sentences before writing some down.

Plenary
Ten minutes before the end of the lesson, bring the children together to share their work with each other. Revise what is an apostrophe and what it looks like. Write two full words such as 'he will' and ask them to write down on a piece of paper how to write it in its shortened version – *he'll*.

Check to see if the children have used the apostrophe in the right place and taken out the correct letters.

Support
Play more matching and pairing games so that the children can verbally and visually recognise contractions vs. their full words.

Extension
Let the children write a short letter that uses contractions. When they have finished let them read it out then read it again by replacing the contractions with the full words. Discuss how the letter sounds and how one is more friendly and said as spoken and the other more formal.

Find the words and contractions

she'll	I am	I'm	she did
isn't	she'd	it is	I had
he had	we're	they've	we are
it's	is not	I'd	she will
he will	he'd	he'll	they have

Match the words and contractions

Name _____

Draw a line to match the words with their contractions.

it is	we're
he will	I'd
I am	he'd
we are	isn't
she will	it's
I had	he'll
they have	she'll
is not	they've
he had	I'm

Search the bag

Name _____

Search the bag to match the full form to its shortened form (contraction).

Saying the words aloud will help.

Full form	Contraction
it is	
he will	
where is	
I am	
we are	
she will	
they have	
is not	
he had	
who has	

Assessment

Contents

Periodic Assessment tests

Test 1 – Nouns   169

Test 2 – Nouns   171

Test 1 – Pronouns   173

Test 2 – Pronouns   175

Test 1 – Verbs   177

Test 2 – Verbs   179

Test 1 – Adjectives   181

Test 2 – Adjectives   183

Test 1 – Sentences   185

Test 2 – Sentences   187

Test 1 – Punctuation   189

Test 2 – Punctuation   191

Transitional Assessment tests

Transitional test 1   193

Transitional test 2   200

Periodic Assessment test 1 – Nouns

Name: _____

Date: _____

Class: _____

Level: _____

1. Which word is the odd one out? Circle the word that is not a noun.

dog   jumping   shop   cup

2. Underline the nouns in the sentences.

   a. The cat ran away.

   b. I went to the park.

   c. I have lost a sock.

   d. The clown was funny.

3. Circle the proper nouns.

   a. I was born in May.

   b. My best friend is called Becky.

   c. I went to London and saw Big Ben.

4. Re-write the proper nouns with a capital letter.

emily   _____

harry   _____

sunday   _____

world cup _____

tesco   _____

5. Match the two words and write their compound nouns.

arm   sun   foot   ball   chair   flower

a. _____

b. _____

c. _____

6. Write the compound nouns from the noun words and pictures.

a.

hand   +   bag   = _____

b.

Jelly   +   fish   = _____

7. Turn these nouns into plurals (more than one thing).

shell_____   boot_____   fox_____   dress_____

8. Add a plural ('-es' or '-s') to the nouns in the sentences.

a. The girl lost two pen_____.

b. The giant put on his shoe _____.

c. Billy got both the torch_____.

9. Add these suffixes to the end of the words to make three new nouns.

'-er'   '-ness'   '-ment'

a.   walk _____

b.   sad _____

c.   pay _____

10. Add a describing word before each of the noun words.

a. _____ butterfly

b. _____ coat

c. _____ lion

Periodic Assessment test 2 – Nouns

Name: _____

Date: _____

Class: _____

Level: _____

1. Underline the common nouns in these sentences.

    a. Joe went to the river and caught a fish.

    b. The alien flew to the blue planet.

    c. The frog jumped on a rock.

2. Add nouns to complete the sentences.

    a. I ran down the _____.

    b. In the jungle I saw a huge hairy _____.

    c. Have you met my _____.

    d. I am off to swim at the _____.

3. Underline the proper nouns in the sentence. Circle the capital letters.

    a. I live along King's Street.

    b. My uncle is going to Canada.

    c. Thea's party is next Saturday.

    d. Mrs Brooks runs the Jumping Gym Club.

4. Write two sentences using these proper nouns.   Shrek   Australia

_____

_____

5. Match the nouns to make and write four compound nouns.

cow   rain   lip   hand stick   bag   boy   bow

_____   _____

_____   _____

6. Write two sentences using these compound nouns.

_____

_____

7. Write the plurals of the nouns in the box.

shell	shells
box	
plate	
beach	
flower	
princess	

8. Turn the nouns in the sentences into plurals.

a. Katy put the stone _____ on her sandcastle.

b. Dad washed the cup _____ and dish_____.

c. Maya has four brush _____ and two comb_____.

9. Add these suffixes to the end of the words to make three new nouns.

'-er'   '-ness'   '-ment'
play   happy   pave

a. _____

b. _____

c. _____

10. Make a noun phrase by adding words before and after the nouns.

a. _____ car_____

b. _____ lion _____

Periodic Assessment test 1 – Pronouns

Name: _____

Date: _____

Class: _____

Level: _____

1. Circle these pronouns in the sentences.

I	me	my	you	your
she	her	he	him	his

a. I like fish and chips.

b. Nan thinks my picture is great.

c. Do you need me?

d. The book is in your bag.

e. She gave him a present.

f. He loved his new tie.

g. Her present was a tin of beans.

2. Add the missing pronouns.

a. Mia is stuck in the mud. _____ needs a pull.

b. Can I see _____ new marble?

c. The queen opened _____ box.

d. The king wanted _____ bath.

3. Write a short sentence using one of these pronouns.

I   my   she   he

_____

_____

_____

4. Circle these pronouns in the sentences.

we	us	our	your
them	their	they	

a. Joe and I went to the park. We played football.

b. You can't catch us!

c. This is our new house.

d. "We love your UFO," they said to the aliens.

e. The hens laid their eggs.

f. The sweets were gone. Who had eaten them?

5. Add the missing pronouns.

a. Can we go to the shops?

b. This is our tent.

c. Their door is red and blue.

d. Jack and Jill fell and the bucket fell behind them.

6. Write a short sentence using one of these pronouns.

we   our   they

_____

_____

_____

_____

_____

Periodic Assessment test 2 – Pronouns

Name: _____

Date: _____

Class: _____

Level: _____

1. Circle these pronouns in the sentences.

I	me	my	you	your
she	her	he	him	his

   a. Lily cooked a cake. She put icing on top.

   b. Ben has asked me over to play.

   c. Have you seen my yo–yo?

   d. I have found your book.

   e. Nan is taking her dog to the vets.

   f. The king is cross. He wants to take his water wings with him.

2. Change the underlined words into a pronoun. Rewrite the sentence with the pronoun on the lines.

Mrs Shaw put <u>Mrs Shaw's</u> flowers in a vase.

_____

The cowboy threw the <u>cowboy's</u> rope over the cow.

_____

The queen was happy. <u>The queen</u> had found her crown.

_____

My name is Max. Max like to row boats.

_____

3. Put the missing pronouns into the spaces using the pronouns below.

we	us	our	your
them	their	they	

My class and I went on a school trip to the seaside. _____ built lots of sandcastles on

the beach. Some of _____ had flags on top. _____ teacher gave _____ the

prize for the best sandcastle. "_____ castle is very good," she said to _____.

The rest of the class clapped _____ hands.

4. Change the underlined words into a pronoun. Rewrite the sentence with the pronoun on the lines.

Jo and I like ice skating. <u>Jo and I</u> like going fast around the rink.

_____

_____

The knights chased the dragons but <u>the knights</u> lost the dragons.

_____

_____

My brother and I are going to the pantomime. Would you like to come with <u>my brother and me</u>?

_____

_____

5. Write one sentence with one of these pronouns:

our   we   they

_____

_____

_____

_____

Periodic Assessment test 1 – Verbs

Name: _____

Date: _____

Class: _____

Level: _____

1. Some of these words are not action verbs. Circle the odd ones out.

   a. jump   giant   run   skip

   b. hop   read   cat   drink

   c. walk   draw catch cup

2. Underline the verbs in the sentences.

   a. Luke likes to ride his bike.

   b. Look at the rabbit hop!

   c. Fish swim in the sea.

   d. I am going to bounce my ball.

3. Make these verbs past tense by adding '-ed' or '-d'.

wash cook pull dance like bake	washed _____ _____ danced _____ _____

4. Add '-ed' or '-d' to the verbs in sentences.

   a. The farmer pull_____ out the large turnip.

   b. The farmer's wife cook_____ the turnip.

   c. The goat chase_____ the boy.

   d. The worm wiggle_____ under a leaf.

5. Make these verbs present tense by adding '-ing'.

call read look make ride wave	calling _____ _____ making _____ _____

6. Add '-ing' to the verbs in sentences.

a. Sam and I are (to play) _____ football.

b. My dad is (to cook) _____ lunch today.

c. Ella loves (to ride) _____ her new bike.

d. I am (to write) _____ a letter to my auntie.

7. Colour in each pair of irregular verbs with a different colour.

dig	see	make	fall
made	fell	dug	saw

8. Add the prefix 'un-' to the verbs.

a. tie _____tie

b. zip _____zip

c. button _____button

Write a sentence using one of the 'un-' verbs.

_____

_____

_____

_____

Periodic Assessment test 2 – Verbs

Name: _____

Date: _____

Class: _____

Level: _____

1. Underline the action verbs in the sentences.

    a. I am going to watch TV later.

    b. Harry went to the tower to ring the bell.

    c. The children had a swim in the sea.

    d. The monkey can swing from tree to tree.

2. Put an action verb in the spaces.

    a. Callum used the bat to _____ the ball.

    b. The girl used her paint brushes to _____ a picture.

    c. Jack and Jill want to _____ down the hill.

    d. The dog began to _____ and _____ his tail.

3. Rewrite these verbs into past tense by adding '-ed' or '-d'.

    bounce _____   chew _____   push _____

    share _____   sail_____   wave _____

4. Write two sentences using these past tense verbs.

    rained   cooked

    _____

    _____

5. Rewrite these verbs into present tense by adding '-ing'.

    read_____   laugh_____   bake_____

    ring_____   love_____   slide_____

6. Add the missing present tense '-ing' verbs to the sentences.

At the Zoo, the lions are roar_____ at the visitors.

The snake is hiss_____ at a boy.

The monkeys are jump_____ up and down.

7. Add the prefix 'un-' to the verbs in the sentences.

a. I must go to my room to _____pack my bag.

b. Can you _____cover the bed.

c. Remember to _____chain your bicycle.

8. Add the right 'to be' verbs before the '-ing' action verbs.

is   am   are   was   were

a. Leo _____ flying his new kite. (present tense)

b. Mo and Sam _____ sailing their model boat. (present)

c. I _____ climbing a tree. (present)

d. Last night, I _____ dancing. (past)

e. Jen and Mum _____ watching me. (past)

9. Draw lines to match the pairs of past and present irregular verbs.

came	sit
told	give
did	come
sat	win
said	tell
won	say
gave	do

Periodic Assessment test 1 – Adjectives

Name: _____

Date: _____

Class: _____

Level: _____

1. One of these words is not an adjective (a describing word). Circle the odd one out.

    a. big   cold   cow   tall

    b. small   hot   wet   ball

    c. dry   leg   white   high

2. Look at the picture of the clown. Put in the adjectives from below in the sentences to show what he looks like.

spotty

curly

big

round

The clown has a _____ nose.

His hair is _____ .

He has a _____ mouth.

He has a _____ hat.

3. Add the prefix 'un-' to these adjectives.

a. happy   _____happy

b. well   _____well

c. helpful   _____helpful

4. Add the prefix 'un-' to the right three describing words.

a. _____lucky   b. _____ rich   c. _____wise

d. _____beautiful   e. _____poor   f. _____kind.

5. Add these suffixes to the end of the words to make adjectives:.

'-ful'   **'-less'**

a. mouth_____   b. play_____

c. harm_____   d. home_____

6. Use the suffixes '-er' and '-est' to complete the captions.

This tower is tall.   This tower is tall_____.   This tower is the _____.

Periodic Assessment test 2 – Adjectives

Name: _____

Date: _____

Class: _____

Level: _____

1. Add adjectives to complete the sentences.

haunted   steep   slimy   scary   blue   wet

The rocks were _____ and _____.

From the top of the _____ hill, Ben could see the _____ sea.

The _____ castle was very _____.

2. Circle the adjectives you would like to use to describe a planet.

The rocket touched down on the rocky / grassy ground. Two orange / purple suns shone their

hot / cold rays onto the planet. A dusty / foggy track led to a large / small lake. Next to it was a

lovely / scary looking alien city.

3. Use some of these adjectives to write three sentences describing an alien. Draw a picture of it in the box.

friendly   slimy   scary   soft   scaly   two   three   hairy   large   loud   shy

four   googly   fat   tall   short   thin   quiet   small   spotty

_____

_____

_____

4. Add the prefix 'un-' to the adjectives in the sentences.

a. Prince Tam was _____ happy about meeting Don the Dragon.

b. He felt _____ well and _____ fit.

c. He knew today could be his _____ lucky day.

5. Rewrite these words by adding one of the suffixes onto the ends.

'-ful'   **'-less'**

a. beauty   _____

b. penny   _____

c. wonder   _____

d. pain   _____

6. Turn these adjectives into adverbs (describes verbs) by adding '-ly'. Remember the '-y'!

a. hopeful_____   b. quick_____   c. slow_____   d. happy_____

Write a sentence using one of the '-ly' words.

_____

7. Fill in the chart

adjective	'-er'	'-est'
big		
		smallest
	tinier	
sad		

Use one of the adjective groups to write a sentence.

_____

_____

_____

Periodic Assessment test 1 – Sentences

Name: _____

Date: _____

Class: _____

Level: _____

1. Add the missing capital letters and full stops.

    a. my mum is making a cup of tea

    b. the boy jumped out of the tree

    c. i have lost my ring

2. Use three colour pencils to match the two parts of simple sentences.

The lollipop lady	are going to the fair.
Liam and I	was very cross.
The troll	stopped the cars.

3. Underline the joining words in the sentences.

    a. Molly put the kettle on and she ate some cake.

    b. I can come to tea but I must ask my mum.

    c. I am tired so I will go to bed.

4. Add 'and' to join the sentences.

    a. An elephant has very large ears _____ a long trunk.

    b. Snails have shells on their back _____ they move very slowly.

5. Add a joining word to join up the two sentences.

and	but	or

I like pasta _____ I do not like rice.

Do I need my boots _____ do I need my shoes?

I am going to see a film _____ Callan is going to see a play.

6. Underline the time words

First I put my boots on.

Then I put my coat on.

Next I put my hat on.

Finally I put my scarf on.

7. Add the time words to the sentences. Draw pictures to go with each sentence.

First	Then	Next	Finally	Later on

_____I dig a hole.

_____I put the seeds in the hole.

_____I put the earth back.

_____I water the seeds.

_____ the seeds grow into flowers.

Periodic Assessment test 2 – Sentences

Name: _____

Date: _____

Class: _____

Level: _____

1. Add capital letters and full stops to show the five sentences in the story.

hetty went to see her auntie for a cup of tea at her auntie's house she saw a bear hiding in the

bushes hetty ran inside to tell her auntie they went outside to find it but the bear had gone all they

found was a big jar of honey.

2. Number these sentences to show the right order.

She went to England to help nurse people.

After the war she was given medals.

Mary Seacole was born in 1805.

She then went to the Crimean War to nurse soldiers.

As a girl she wanted to be a nurse.

3. Underline a joining word in the sentences.

a. I want to climb the hill but my foot is sore.

b. The mouse nibbled the cheese and then he fell asleep.

c. The car broke down so I walked to school.

4. Add the right joining word.

and	but	so	or

a. I could eat the carrots _____ I could eat the peas.

b. Davy like oranges _____ he does not like apples.

c. The sea was blue _____ the sand was yellow.

d. I have a cold _____ I can't come.

5. Add a joining word to join up the extra information.

because	if	that	when	

a.   Captain Zoom headed back to Earth _____ he heard about the aliens.

b.   He had to get there quickly _____ he was to stop them.

c.   He was nervous _____ the aliens were scary.

d.   He landed in a wood _____ was close to the aliens' UFO.

6. Use one of the joining words to write a sentence about what happened next.
Main part of the sentence + joining word + extra information.

_____

_____

_____

_____

_____

_____

_____

7. Add the missing time words (time connectives).

first	then	next	finally	later on

_____ we put on our coats and boots.

_____we walked to the bonfire.

_____ we watched the bonfire.

_____we watched the fireworks.

_____we had hot soup and rolls.

Periodic Assessment test 1– Punctuation

Name: _____

Date: _____

Class: _____

Level: _____

1. Add the missing capital letters and full stops to the sentences.

a.   on monday i like swimming

b.   on tuesday i like dancing

c.   on wednesday i like singing

d.   on thursday i like climbing

e.   on friday i like shopping

f.   on saturday i like riding

What do you like doing on Sunday?

I like _____

2. Add the question marks to the questions.

a. What is your name

b. How old are you

c. Where do you live

d. Who is your best friend

e. When were you born

3. Draw a line to match the answers to the questions.

<u>What</u> is a baby lion called?   My birthday is in May.

How many legs has a spider?   An apple is green.

Where is Big Ben?   A baby lion is called a cub.

Who was Mary Seacole?   A spider has eight legs.

When is your birthday?   Big Ben is in London.

Which is green, a carrot or an apple?   Mary Seacole was a nurse.

4. Add exclamation marks (!) to the right sentences.

Look out   Tea time   Help   I like chips

5. Add commas to the list.

For my birthday I got a robot   socks   paints   a book   a bike and a CD.

6. Make a list out of these words and add commas.

monkey   snake   lion   goat   and a hippo.

At the zoo I saw _____

_____

_____

_____

_____

7. Fill in the chart.

Words	Contractions
I will	I'll
I am	
We will	
He will	
We are	
She had	

Periodic Assessment test 2 – Punctuation

Name: _____

Date: _____

Class: _____

Level: _____

1. Add the missing capital letters and full stops to these instructions.

<u>how to clean a car</u>

a.   fill a bucket of water from the tap   b.   put a soap called carshine in the water

c.   soak the cloth   d.   wash the car all over with the soapy water

e.   use clean water to wash the soap off   f.   polish the car with a dry cloth

2. Write the questions to these answers.

_____

A baby horse is called a foal.

_____

I am seven years old.

_____

This egg was laid by a dinosaur.

_____

I would like to eat curry and rice.

3. Complete these questions with your own words. Underline the question words.

a. Where is the _____

b. Who is your _____

c. When can you _____

d. How does a _____

e. What is a _____

f. Which games do you _____

4. Add exclamation marks (!) to the right sentences.

a. This gift is beautiful

b. The horse is hungry

c. The aliens are coming

d. I like a cup of tea

5. Add commas to this list.

When I went to the party dressed as an explorer I wore heavy boots   waterproof trousers   a coat

a warm hat   a stripy scarf and a pair of gloves.

6. Make a list using some of these words.

brushes   glue   paint   scissors   pencils   paper

In the art cupboard there are _____

_____

_____

_____

7. Add the apostrophe (') in the right place for the word contractions. Write out the full words next to the contractions.

I ll   = I will

a. We ll = _____

b. I m = _____

c. We re = _____

Transitional Assessment test 1

Name: _____

Date: _____

Class: _____

Level: _____

Common nouns
Circle the words that are nouns.

car	funny	pirate	house	run	ball
clown	school	cow	sad	cry	lion

Proper nouns
Give the proper nouns in the sentences a capital letter.

a. My teacher is called mrs gaskin.

b. I went to devon for my holiday.

c. Tomorrow is monday.

d. My brother is called leo.

Common nouns and proper nouns
Underline the proper nouns in the sentences. Circle the common nouns in the sentences.

a. We stayed in a caravan at Sunny Days Park.

b. My uncle lives in Canada.

c. The bus stops at the High Street.

d. I bought a hat at Hatters.

Compound nouns
Write the three compound nouns beginning with 'foot'.

_____

_____

_____

Plural nouns ending with '-s' and '-es'
Turn these nouns into plurals. Use one to write a short sentence.

elephant___   drum_____   fox_____   coach_____

_____

Making nouns with suffixes
Add the suffixes '-ness', '-ment' or '-er ' to the words.

a.   dark_____

b.   paint_____

c.   amaze_____

Expanded noun phrases
Add words in front of the noun to describe it.

_____ dog.

Singular pronouns

I	my	you	your
she	he	him	his

Circle the pronouns in the sentences.

a. This is my best friend, Lulu.

b. She is so funny.

c. Your mum has cooked me a cake.

d. Harvey fell on his knees.

e. He did not want him to go.

f. I hope you can come to my party.

Plural Pronouns

we	they	our
them	their	

Underline the pronouns in the sentences.

a. We are going to the circus.

b. Some people were in our seats.

c. Their seats were in another row.

d. They got up and moved to them.

Action verbs
Add the action verbs to the missing spaces.

jump   push   cut   sing

a. Tim _____ the paper up.

b. Megan likes to _____ songs.

c. Dad had to _____ the car.

d. Let's _____ on my bed.

Past tense verbs ending in '-ed'
Turn these into verbs into past tense using '-ed' or '-d'.

play_____   dance_____

Use the verbs to write two short sentences.

_____

_____

Present tense verbs ending in '-ing'
Rewrite these verbs into present tense using '-ing'.

help _____   save _____

Use the '-ing' verbs to write two short sentences.

_____

_____

Progressive verbs
Underline the 'to be' verbs with one colour pencil and the '-ing' action verbs with another colour pencil.

is   am   are   was   were

a.   The farmer is driving the tractor.

b.   The cows were eating the grass.

c.   I am cooking tea.

d.   We are having a picnic.

Using the prefix 'un-' with verbs
Add the prefix 'un-' to the verbs. Write your own at the end.

_____ tie   _____chain   _____do   un_____

Irregular verbs
Draw a line to match the verbs.

see
fall
run

fell
ran
saw

End the sentences in your own words.

a. I can see _____

b. I saw _____

Descriptive adjectives
Write the adjectives next to the right nouns.

cold   hot   dry   blue   rocky

__ __ __ __ sea   __ __ __ __ snow   __ __ __ sun

__ __ __ __ __ hills   __ __ __ desert

Descriptive adjectives
Use some of the adjectives to fill in the sentences about this superhero.

long   short   spotty

spiky   funny   great   silly

She is wearing a _____ skirt.

She has _____ boots.

Her hair is _____.

I think she is _____.

Using the 'un-' prefix for adjectives
Add the prefix 'un-' to these adjectives. Add your own 'un-' word at the end.

a. kind   _____

b. wise   _____

c. happy   _____

d. _____

Making adjectives and adverbs with suffixes
Use a red pencil to colour in the words that mean tall.
Use a blue pencil to colour in the words that mean small.

'-ful'   '-less'   '-ly'

a. care_____   b. hope_____

c. use_____   d. love_____

Simple sentences
Write the mixed up words in the right order.

put kettle on. the Polly

_____

Compound sentences – joining words
Put in the right joining words.

and	but	or

a. The cat chased the dog _____ the dog chased the mouse.

b. The mouse ran up the tree _____ the dog ran into the tree.

c. Did the mouse get away _____ did the dog get away?

d. _____

Joining extra information to a sentence
Put in the right joining words.

because	if	when

a. I love eating honey _____it is so runny.

b. I will come round today _____you are in.

c. I saw the queen _____ we went to London.

Time words (Time connectives)
Underline the time words.

First I beat the eggs.

Then I put the bread in the eggs.

Next I fry the bread.

Finally it is cooked.

Capital letters and full stops
Add the missing capital letters and full stops to the two sentences.

a.   on monday we are going to visit juppton zoo

b.   look at that picture of queen victoria

Questions
Add question marks to these questions.

a. Where is the park

b. Who is going to pick up the bean bags

c. How do you make a cup of tea

d. Why did the hen cross the road

Commas in lists
Add commas to the two lists.

In my bedroom there is a bed a rug books   a toy box   a lamp and my teddy.

At the seaside I saw a crab   a seagull a sandcastle a shell and seaweed.

Apostrophes – contractions
Add the apostrophes to the word contractions.

I ll   she d   we ll   he s   it s

Transitional Assessment test 2

Name: _____

Date: _____

Class: _____

Level: _____

Common nouns
Write a sentence about each common noun.

octopus   school   fire–fighter   hat

_____

_____

_____

_____

Proper nouns
There is something wrong with the proper nouns in these sentences.
Re-write them correctly in the spaces.

Have you seen tom (_____)? We need to go to the

cinema to see toy story (_____).

Common nouns and proper nouns
Write the proper noun answers to the common nouns in the box below.

My name.	_____
The town or village where I live.	_____
My favourite day of the week.	_____

Compound nouns
Add nouns to the spaces to make compound nouns.

a. hand _____   b. arm _____

c. butter _____   d. ear _____

e. knee _____   f. key _____

Plural nouns
Fill in the spaces to make plural nouns.

Jack ran down the road to buy some sticky doughnut_____. In the bakery he also bought four fairy

cake_____, three jam tart_____ and six cheese straw_____. The baker wanted ten gold

coin____ but Jack only had two magic bean_____.

Plural nouns with '-s' or '-es'
Write out the plural nouns to these singular nouns.

wish   torch   box

_____   _____   _____

dress   rose   bear

_____   _____   _____

Making nouns with suffixes
Add in the suffixes '-ness' , '-ment' or '-er ' to the words in the sentences.

a.   The party was filled with happy   _____.

b.   One day I would like to be a climb _____.

c.   Dad tripped over the broken pave _____.

Expanded noun phrases
Add words in front of the noun to describe it and after it to show where it is.

_____ house_____.

Singular pronouns

I	me	my	you	your
she	her	he	him	his

Put in the missing pronouns.

Chloe went into lunch with _____ class. "Can _____ sit with _____?

"asked Jacob. Jacob took out _____ lunch. "_____ mum has given _____ a lot

of food," he said. "What have you got?" Chloe looked at _____. "Worms!" _____ laughed.

Plural Pronouns

we	us	our
them	their	they

Underline the pronouns in the sentences.

Joe and I heard a bang. We looked out of our window. Aliens had landed in our garden. We gave them a cup of tea. Then they went back to their UFOs and zoomed off.

Saying verbs
Write three sentences using three of these saying verbs.

asked   begged   cried   moaned   shouted   laughed   whispered   yawned   sighed

_____

_____

_____

Past tense verbs ending in '-ed' or '-d'
Turn the verbs into past tense verbs.

a. Billy bounce_____ up and down on the trampoline.

b. Francis Drake sail_____ around the world.

c. Leah looked at the picture and giggle_____.

d. Pirate Pip slowly turn_____ the key to the treasure chest.

Present tense verbs ending in '-ing'
Rewrite the verbs into present tense verbs adding '-ing'.

ride _____   ring _____

hide _____   skate_____

Use two of the present tense verbs to write two sentences.

_____

_____

Progressive form of verbs
Add the right 'to be' verbs before the '-ing' action verbs.

is   am   are   was   were

a.   The thief _____ running away. (present)

b.   We _____ going on holiday. (present)

c.   I _____ swimming.(present)

d.   The dog _____ barking at the postman. (past)

e.   Mum and Dad _____ laughing. (past)

Using 'un-' prefix for verbs
Add the prefix 'un-' to the verbs in the sentences.

a.   Will you _____plug the light?

b.   I can't _____screw this jar!

c.   I need the key to _____lock the door.

Present tense or past tense verbs
Use a red pencil to colour in the sentences which are in past tense.
Use a blue pencil to colour in the sentences which are in present tense.

I am hiding under the bed.	We laughed at the clown.	Mum is baking a cake.
Viv has painted the gate.	I jumped into a puddle.	The dog barked at the cat.

Irregular verbs
Add the correct irregular verbs to the sentences.

dig   dug   give   gave   took   take

a.   The builder is going to _____ a hole in the road.

b.   The pirate _____ up a treasure chest.

c.   I am going to _____ my mum a hug.

d.   Emma _____ Jacob a new model car.

e.   Our teacher is going to _____ us swimming.

f.   I _____ my computer game with me.

Descriptive adjectives
Add adjectives to end the sentences.

The beach was very _____.

The grass was very _____.

The sun was very _____.

The snow was very _____.

Descriptive adjectives
Write a description of a story book character using some of these adjectives.

happy	sad	large	tall	small	little	kind	nasty	ugly	pretty	
brave	scary	shy	quiet	noisy	funny	angry	clever	stupid		

_____

_____

_____

_____

Using 'un-' prefix for adjectives
Add the prefix 'un-' to the adjective. Write the meanings of the adjective and 'un-' adjective.

Selfish _____selfish

selfish means _____.

____selfish means _____.

Making adjectives and adverbs with suffixes
Add these suffixes to the end of the words in the sentences.

'-ful'   '- less'   '-ly'

a.   This baking tool will be really use_____.

b.   The large giant was so care_____.

c.   The tortoise calm_____ and slow_____ walked across the line.

Verb suffixes '-er' and '-est'
Use the suffixes '-er' and '-est' for these adjectives.

quiet   loud

This mouse is quiet.   This mouse is _____.

This mouse is the _____.

This _____ is loud. This _____ is louder.

This _____ is the loudest.

Simple sentences
Write the mixed up words in the right order.

shoemaker The man. a poor very was

_____

fireworks the We sky. the sparkle in saw

_____

Write your own sentence about Bonfire Night.

_____

_____

_____

Compound sentence
Add the missing joining words of the compound sentences.

and	but	or	so

a. Josh kicked the ball _____ it went in the goal.

b. I can go to the park _____ I can play in the garden.

c. Harry came to see his Gran _____ the lift was broken.

d. The book fell on the floor _____ Lily picked it up.

Joining extra information to a sentence
Add a joining word to give the extra information.

because	if	when

a.   I like eating apples _____ they are crunchy.

b.   There will be no school tomorrow _____ it snows.

c.   I will make you a pizza _____ you come to tea.

Time connectives
Complete the sentences that start with time connectives to describe your day.

First _____

_____

Then _____

_____

Next _____

_____

Finally _____

_____

Full stops and exclamation marks
Add the missing full stops or exclamation marks to the sentences.

a.   Watch out for that boomerang

b.   Lots of castles have moats around them

c.   Look at that huge fish

d.   I like going to my street dance lessons

Questions
Write the questions to the animal answers.

_____

Kangaroos come from Australia.

_____

The tallest animal is the giraffe.

_____

The snail has a shell for a home.

_____

The fastest animal in the world is the cheetah.

Commas in lists
Add commas to the list.

You can have strawberry   chocolate   vanilla lemon   coconut or cherry ice cream.

Write a list of your five favourite foods.

_____

_____

_____

_____

Apostrophes – contractions
Add the contractions in the right place.

He'll   it's   we're   I'm   they're

a. (He will) _____get hurt if he is not careful.

b. (It is) _____over the hill and down the lane.

c. (I am) _____ so tired!

d. (They are) _____ away at the seaside.

e. (We are)_____ having a great time!

Notes